PENGUIN BOOKS
BBC BOOKS

THE TROTTER WAY TO MILLIONS

Born and bred in Nelson Mandela House, Peckham's answer to the Trump Tower, Derek 'Del Boy' Trotter has been doing business for longer than all of Richard Branston's pullovers put together.

The first yuppie to drive a yellow three-wheeler, Derek is now the chairman and chief executive of TITCO (TROTTERS INDEPENDENT TRADING COMPANY). Call it killer instinct, call it *servir frais mais non glacé*, Del Trotter had what it took to go right to the top. Having finally reached the penthouse, he says the Tia Maria-and-Lucozades are on him.

Engaged more times than a switchboard and at one time Peckham's most illegible bachelor, Derek recently became its proudest father when his long-term relationship with Raquel produced Damian, heir to the TITCO empire.

Only Fools and Horses

THE TROTTER WAY
TO MILLIONS

THINGS THEY ONLY TEACH YOU AT
THE *Peckham Business School*

by Derek Trotter *as told to John Haselden*
Based on the BBC TV series by John Sullivan

PENGUIN BOOKS
BBC BOOKS

For Mark Hopkinson, an old mucker who went offshore

PENGUIN BOOKS
BBC BOOKS

Published by the Penguin Group and BBC Enterprises Ltd
Penguin Books Ltd, 27 Wrights Lane, London w8 5tz, England
Penguin Books USA Inc., 375 Hudson Street, New York, New York 10014, USA
Penguin Books Australia Ltd, Ringwood, Victoria, Australia
Penguin Books Canada Ltd, 10 Alcorn Avenue, Toronto, Ontario,
Canada m4v 3b2
Penguin Books (NZ) Ltd, 182–190 Wairau Road, Auckland 10, New Zealand

Penguin Books Ltd, Registered Offices: Harmondsworth, Middlesex,
England

First published by BBC Books, a division of BBC Enterprises Ltd, 1990
Published by Penguin Books and BBC Books,
a division of BBC Enterprises, 1994
10 9 8 7 6 5 4 3 2 1

Typeset by Datix International Limited, Bungay, Suffolk
Printed in England by Clays Ltd, St Ives plc

CONTENTS

....

ACKNOWLEDGEMENTS

....

Apart from Mum, my old partner Jumbo Mills and Mike at the Nag's Head, I'd like to thank John Haselden, who wrote this book in my own words, leaving me free to carry on outing the merchandise.

My editor, Sheila Ableman, I call Miss 999, 'cos she's always there in emergencies.

Sir John Harvey-Oswald helped steer the Good Ship TITCO through a bit of fiscal turbulence.

Andy McMorrin, a graduate from the Hendon Business School, provided much inspiration.

Nick Chapman and Chris Weller are, quite simply, the *crème de la menthe*.

I owe a great debt to our friends at Customs and Excise, but they're very busy people and I never like to bother them.

And to my brother Rodney, who's dropped enough major gooleys over the years to virtually skint the Trotter empire, I'd like to say: '*You plonker!*'

FOREWORD *by Sir John Harvey-Jones*

It is not every day of the week that a chap like me gets an opportunity like this—a once-and-for-all, un-repeatable (or so I understand it to be) chance to speak up for TITCO and all that it means to so many of us.

When I was first asked to write this foreword I confess to feeling dead chuffed, or one, or the other. Later, when I realized the task I had undertaken, I became reassured and buoyed up with the expectation of the unique case, for I understand only one was fabricated, of Costa Rican champagne I have been promised as a *pour boire* or a *pour* something or possibly just plain poor.

How can I do justice to Mr Trotter, where so many have been trying to do so, for so long, with such signal lack of success? Here is a businessman who has done everything and everyone. I have been asked, incidentally, if any reader has not yet encountered one of Mr Trotter's varied activities, would he or she be kind enough to forward details of their interest and current bank balance (accompanied in the case of ladies by a recent photograph) to the International Headquarters at Peckham. They can expect immediate personal attention. Not that you should be in any way misled as to the type of personal service you may expect from TITCO. Their interests are more in doing you than the opposite.

The reader who delves into the deeper details of this book will learn a great deal they don't teach at the Harvard Business School or for that matter at Wapping Polytechnic. For here is revealed, for the first time, experiences of business life that only so ubiquitous and questing an operator as Mr Trotter can gather and garnish. No deal is too complex for him—no profit is too small, or even too unlikely, to gather his attention. Just as the TITCOs of this world come in all sizes and shapes, and seldom fail to attract the attention of businessmen of every type, so do Mr Trotter's interests. In addition, he has an apparently limitless willingness to try the new—to go where no businessman has gone before, and the few that have have all too often not returned—at least for periods of six months to two years maximum.

It is said that no matter how skilful one is, no one can succeed without able supporters and a share of luck. If there is one word of criticism, it is that Del Trotter does not always seem to me to address the problems of selection and management training with the success that his undoubted interests in these areas could possibly bring.

Nobody could fault his attempts at delegation. But, sadly, one has the feeling that his staff are not always with him, so to speak. As for his luck—well, the record speaks for itself. A nationally famous brand name, an international range of interests, an unusual period headquarters building: all of these things speak for themselves or not at all.

I wish the reader every success. Mr Trotter will, as he always has, continue to make his own.

John Harvey-Coom

A NOTE ON THE *Peckham Business School*

A while back, I went down the local library and read some ancient manuscripts written by the elders of Peckham. You know, five hundred years ago you would have been able to look out the window of Nelson Mandela House, the present-day headquarters of the Trotter Independent Trading Company, and behold a green and pleasant environmental area. The Earl of Peckham had a castle where the Kwikfit Exhaust Centre now stands. Flaxen-haired maidens used to dance around the village maypole of an evening.

Then, one fateful medieval day, the Trotter clan arrived in a stolen Zephyr. Before you knew it, the flaxen-haired maidens were up the spout, the old earl had been sold some hookey armour and someone nicked the maypole. Out of this series of apparently unconnected events the fundamental principles of the Peckham Business School were born.

A hundred years later, the Black Death arrived and the earl was in deep stuke. He'd dropped a bundle to

Sir Reginald Trotter and his squire, Boycie, at an all-night tournament. Whilst Sir Reg refused on a point of honour to take the earl's IOU, he was prepared to meet him half-way. He bestowed upon the earl a smallholding behind the khazi in the Nag's Head car-park, accepting for himself the deeds to the entire SE15 postal district and a bevy of flaxen-haired maidens for business and personal use.

By the early 1950s the flaxen-haired maidens had been round the track more times than a lurcher, but the Business School was walloping along. It had become the jewel in the crown of the University of Hard Knocks.

You can't just ponce around in a tee-shirt at the PBS. A Bulgarian three-piece suit is your uniform, the sort of gear that says you're ready to do the business. The streets are its campus, the saloon bar at the Nag's Head its lecture hall.

Now, for the first time, I'm offering you, the punter, the exclusive opportunity to discover its secrets in the comfort of your own boardroom.

Do you, like me, have a hankering for the esoteric things in life? Are you dead set on ironing out those wrinkles in your management style? Have you ever been saddled with a brother who's a complete dipstick as a financial adviser?

Well, make yourself a Singapore Swing and a ham sandwich, pull a swivel chair up in front of the TV, put a bit of Chekhov on the stereo, and *read on* . . .

INTRODUCTION

....

Dave Trump, Lee Hokeycokey, Del Trotter. If each of us was to put fifty pence in a jam jar every time a punter asks: 'How do you do it?', this time next year we'd be millionaires.

I'm the first to agree with Dave when he says it's not as easy as it looks in the global market these days. No matter what you've got pugged away for a rainy day—a medallion out of place, the wrong aftershave, a bird doing her pieces all over the front page of the *Peckham Gazette* is all it takes. Before you know it even the VAT man don't want your autograph.

This is where *The Trotter Way to Millions* comes in. It don't matter if you're on your way to your first million or on your way back—this book is for you. As Sir John Harvey-Oswald said when he'd finished the manuscript: 'Del, this ain't a classic, it's a bleeding millstone!' I couldn't have put it better myself.

Whether it's knocking out pirate videos down the market (*Treasure Island*, *Mutiny on the Bounty*, you name it) or presentation sets of Henry VIII's skull to the

Americans (the large one is him as a king, the small one, him as a boy) each of my ideas is guaranteed to stand apart from the conventional business opportunities you often read about.

What's more, I invite you, the reader, to join me in a privileged glimpse of the fantastic bargains that lurk within the House of Trotter, *all available on easy terms!* So, prepare to enter a different world, and remember: the Trotter 'Can't Lose' Guarantee protects you!

But I'll level with you. I can't promise that any one scheme will bring you overnight success. Especially if you've got a brother called Rodney. But if you're not *absolutely delighted* with *The Trotter Way to Millions*, complain to the publishers. Something is probably wrong with the cover, or they forgot to poof-read it or something, the plonkers. It's got nothing to do with me.

My business methods are almost mythical. All right, I have been let down by my suppliers from time to time and been forced to shift the odd bit of dodgy merchandise, but I've rarely failed to teach most of those I've dealt with a lesson they will never forget, and many have made a fortune by listening to my tips and suggestions—especially at the poker table.

Not that I'm a gambling man. The financial market is about forty-two-carrot, blue-chip investments; it's a place for specialists, and I specialize in everything.

From superior objets d'art to cheap washing powder, the TITCO warehouse has counted it all out.

Part autobiography, part business manual and all success story, *The Trotter Way to Millions* seeks to inspire by example. Whether you want the lowdown on GOING OFFSHORE, a new slant on THE JAPANESE CHALLENGE or to follow my environmentally friendly footsteps in CLEANING UP; if you're keen to sharpen up the corporate profile, pull the right class of bramma or remind yourself of the importance of traditional values, Del Trotter's your man. Each section draws from a wealth of incident and personal anecdote to highlight a vital and far-reaching business lesson.

With characteristic frankness, I tell you not only what lay behind my many triumphs, but in some cases who lay in front of them. Yes, I also analyse, almost brutally, the reason for my occasional failures. I hope this method will be instructive to my many readers—and to Rodney in particular.

But *The Trotter Way to Millions* is not just a business book. It's also about philosophy, my philosophy of success. Let me give you a for instance. Diamond smuggling. It's only illegal 'cos Boycie and his partner Abdul ain't paying import tax on them. Now, say they paid their import tax. What would the government do with the money? They'd only go and buy another Strident missile, wouldn't they? So smuggling diamonds is a blow for world peace. Common sense, really, I know, but you'd be surprised how few punters take that on board.

The moral is: buy a whole vanload of this book. You'll not only cop an earner, the chances are you'll end up with the Nobel Prize as well!

Del Trotter

DEREK TROTTER

PECKHAM

CHAPTER ONE

Picking the Right Team

Nigel Dawson, Colonel 'Ernie' Sanders, the Driscoll brothers and more or less every other big noise in the business game will be right behind

When going it alone, make sure you pick the right partner. When selecting a financial director, get one with 20/20 vision.

me when I say that it's tough at the top. It takes time, energy and *courgettes nouvelle* to build a trading empire, and you can't go it alone, as Rodders discovered a few years back when he became the victim of a hostile take-over bid from his mucker Mickey Pearce.

Like most of the stories in *The Trotter Way to Millions*, what follows is a bit of a cautionary tale, and I don't mind admitting that I learnt a thing or two along the way.

As it happens, it all began where most things finish up — on the pavement outside Top Shop. I was down there shifting some merchandise while Rodders kept a weather eye out for anything that might interfere with the smooth running of the operation. Or so I thought.

'No, they're beautiful, ain't they?' Quite a few punters were there to witness the Trotter magic, and I was starting to motor. 'I don't care if your nipper's got measles, mumps or a scabby eye, these yap-yap dogs are guaranteed to put a smile back on his face! I'll tell you ladies something, and don't let it go any further 'cos I might be in breach of the Official Secrets Act! Little Prince William's got one of these in his nursery at Buck House. No, honestly, and I'll tell you how I know. His Dad gave me a bell the other week. He said, "Del Boy, I'm in right lumber, the enemy's doing her pieces 'cos I forgot Spud's birthday!" Spud's their nickname for him! So I walloped over there a bit lively with one of these. End of aggravation. End of story!'

There were seven or eight yap-yap dogs doing their number in the open display case in front of me. I was about to shift the lot. I could see Rodney at the street corner, slack-jawed with admiration. Mind you, he quite often looks like that when he's thinking.

'Each one comes complete with batteries and is guaranteed house-trained! And this is none of your Taiwan or Hong Kong rubbish either.' I pointed to the label. 'There you are: "Made in Burma"! Now what can't speak can't lie!'

I moved in for the kill. 'The recommended retail

price of these quality items is fourteen pounds sixty-five! I'm letting you have them for six quid. Now I can't say fairer than that, can I?'

As I prepared to take the money I saw what, had Rodney not been on look-out duty, might easily have passed for a copper's helmet making its way through my clientele.

'Now you may think they're remarkably cheap and you're right! They *are* remarkably cheap! I'm going on holiday soon and I need the suitcase!'

Would you Adam and Eve it? It *was* a copper's helmet, and it was slicing its way towards yours truly like Jaws' younger brother. I decided to pack immediately and take an earlier plane.

There comes a time in every businessman's day when he has to think on his feet. I'm here to tell you it's not always easy, especially when you're shifting through Top Shop at a hundred and twenty with a case full of yap-yap dogs and the Old Bill breathing down your neck. I hadn't even had time to switch off the merchandise. Some of those punters must have thought I was barking.

I made it back to the nerve centre of the Trotter empire by the scenic route. Grandad was catching up on some TV. He noticed I'd arrived when I hurled the suitcase down on the floor of the lounge and gave it some with the toecap of my Gucci loafers.

'Had a good day, Del?' he asked.

'Oh, the best, Grandad, the very bloody best. I have been pursued by a *gendarme*, attacked by Pussycat Willum and almost caught rabies! And it's all this dipstick's fault!'

'You don't half exaggerate!' said the dipstick.

'*Exaggerate?*' I bellowed. 'You should have been down that alley with me, Rodders. Eight yapping dogs in my bag and twenty-eight more of the little bleeders at my heels. It was like *Call of the Wild*! Why didn't you warn me that copper was coming?'

'I didn't see him!'

'You didn't see him! What do you want me to get you, radar?'

'You've got to give him the benefit of the doubt, Del!' Grandad said.

'Thank you, Grandad,' Rodney said. 'At least someone understands!'

The out-of-work lamplighter looked up from *Jackanory* and nodded. 'I mean they are difficult to spot—with their size eighteen boots and big pointed heads!'

That really got Rodney out of his pram.

'Why don't you shut your mouth, you sarky old goat!'

'And what about the other day when we was knocking out them Italian shirts?' I said. 'That wasn't just one copper you failed to warn me about—it was a squad car! It stood there at the kerb, all big and white with a red stripe running through the middle like a tube of Signal!'

Rodney paused. 'I didn't spot it.'

'But you must have been a bit suspicious when this giant jam sandwich pulled up bang next to you . . .'

'Maybe he needs medical help, Del Boy,' suggested Grandad with the benefit of a lifetime's experience.

'Either that or glasses,' I said.

'I've had a lot on my mind recently,' Rodney said. 'I've been struggling to find a way of making a very important announcement! For the last two weeks or so I've been taking stock of my life. Who I am, what I am and where I'm going . . .'

'And that's taken you a fortnight?' I said. 'I could have answered all them questions for you during a commercial break!'

'Will you shut up and listen to me for one moment?' As ever, he had scant regard for the formalities of the boardroom. 'I am twenty-four. I have two GCEs, thirteen years of schooling and three terms at an adult education centre behind me! And with all that, what have I become? I'm a look-out!' He hesitated. 'What I'm trying to say, Del, is . . . I'm thinking of dissolving the partnership . . .'

Constitutionally, of course, he was well out of order, but I opted for the gentle art of persuasion. 'Rodders, you pranny,' I said. 'What do you want to break it up for? We're doing well! Business is booming, profits are up! What more do you want?'

'I want to make my own decisions,' came the riposte. 'I've made one so far today, Del. I'm going it alone.'

'Who with?' I asked.

'Mickey Pearce.'

Mickey Pearce. That really gave my arse a headache. No way was that soppy cod going to pull one over Peckham's answer to Lee Hokeycokey.

'Mickey Pearce couldn't keep a rabbit going with lettuce!'

'Mickey's quite an astute businessman,' Rodney said. 'And he's putting capital into our venture.'

'Oh, he's put money in, has he?'

Rodney hesitated. 'Well, no . . . But he will as soon as his Giro cheque arrives!'

This was hardly my idea of a major Stock Market flirtation.

'And what are you putting up, Rodders?'

'I've got money, Del Boy!'

This was a new one on me.

'I've got my half of the partnership!'

'Partnership? Oh, *our* partnership . . .'

I was facing the sort of board-level crisis that would have given Colonel 'Ernie' Sanders itchy fever. There was no alternative. I had to take decisive action.

'All right, Rodney, if that's the way you want it!' I brought out my wad. The sudden silence in the room was broken only by the riffling of large denomination banknotes. I counted him off a handful of fivers.

'You'd better understand one thing, Rodney. Going it alone means exactly what it says! You pay your own way in the world. You pay your own way in pubs and you pay your own way in this house. You get nothing for nothing. If things don't go the way you want them to I don't want to hear no moaning and whining!'

'I won't moan or whine about nothing!'

I gave him the ackers and he changed his mind.

'Is this all I've got?' he moaned. 'Bloody hell, Del, all these years and you give me this!'

It was time for another lesson in the harsh realities of monetarism. 'Things have been a bit shaky of late . . . Profits are down and—'

'But just now you said we were doing well!' he whined, betraying a touching inability to grasp the big financial picture.

'Relatively speaking, Rodders,' I explained patiently. 'I mean, we are doing well compared with . . . for example . . . an Iranian gin salesman. But Lesson Numero Uno in the market place is: a trader's only as good as his stock—and I bought a lot of stock off Alfie Flowers yesterday.'

'Right, this'll have to do then, won't it?' he said,

stuffing the money defiantly into his anorak pocket. Then he threw down the gimlet: 'I'm going to prove to you that I've got business acumen and that I'm as quickwitted as you! I'll see you at the auction tomorrow!'

'It reminds me of *Dallas*,' Grandad said when Rodney had gone. 'You two are just like Bobby and J.R.!'

I looked in the executive mirror and straightened my medallion. 'Yeah,' I said. 'I suppose I do look a bit like that Bobby Ewing.'

Dave Trump and me have always had a lot in common. For both of us, the deal is not just an art, it's a religion, and the auction room is our place of worship. It's where we dealers come to see and be seen, to display the tomfoolery, to speculate a few chips on life's roulette wheel. On this particular day the air was heavy with the scent of Brut and banknotes. I was ready to roll.

'Lot 35, gentlemen, as you can see from your catalogues, is a consignment of smoke-damaged fire-alarms . . .'

Some things just can't be taught, even at the Peckham Business School. If you ain't born with the scent of the auction room in your blood, you could come out of an athletic discussion looking like a right berk.

As the auctioneer did his number, I looked around
for the dynamic duo. They were hanging around at
the back. Rodney looked like he does at the disco
when he's hoping someone will ask him to dance.
Mickey was twitching so badly I thought he must
have left the pins in his mohair suit. I went over to
give them a bit of advice.

'You've got to be very careful what you do with
your hands at places like this. You probably don't
realize it, Mickey, but just now you put in a forty-
pound bid for an electric generator when you
scratched your bum.'

'Did I?' Mickey said, with the look of a man whose
Giro cheque is still in the post.

'He's winding you up!' Rodney's eyeballs disap-
peared into the top of his head.

'What are you after?' I asked.

'The cut-glass goblets,' Mickey said, playing his
cards very close to his chest.

'No, we're not,' said Rodney.

'But I thought you—'

'No, no,' Rodney said, cool as a cucumber. 'We
ain't after nothing in particular.'

'Here,' I said, 'the one to beware of today is
Lot 37. It's little more than a load of scrap iron, so be
careful!'

I was out in the yard with Harry the foreman when I

next saw Peckham's answer to Satchel and Satchel. They were standing by a pile of rusty lawnmower engines looking like turkeys who'd just caught Bernard Matthews grinning at them. At the top of the heap was a ticket saying Lot 37.

'You bought this, son?' Harry said.

'Yeah.' Rodney squirmed.

Harry started to laugh. 'There's one at every auction, ain't there, Del?'

'Except when there's two, Harry,' I said.

Rodney stormed over to me as I was loading Lot 36 into the van.

'We've bought a load of rubbish!'

'I did try to warn you, Rodders,' I said.

'Yeah, but I thought . . .'

'That is your trouble, Rodney, you will insist on thinking.'

As I locked the back of the van he nodded towards the contents. 'What have you got?'

To laugh then would not have been in keeping with the gravity of the occasion. I tried to save it for later. 'I picked up those crystal goblets you were after.'

'What *are* these things?' Mickey yelled, pointing at the Pearce Partnership's first entry into the profit-and-loss account.

'They're lawnmower engines,' I said.

'Lawnmower engines?' Rodney asked.

'But they're no ordinary lawnmower engines,' I

said, settling into the driver's seat of TITCO's motor fleet. 'They're broken lawnmower engines.'

As I gunned the Reliant's engine, Rodney leaned through the window.

'Er, Del . . . We're going to have a few headaches getting this gear back to our, um . . . depot . . .'

'Yeah,' Mickey said. 'We came down on the Green Line, see . . .'

I appraised the situation. 'Your best bet is to hire an open-backed truck.'

'Well, we was wondering if we could put a few of them in the back of the van.'

'You must be joking, Rodders,' I said. 'I've only just cleared them out of the van.'

It took a moment or two for Rodney to warm up the software on this. 'You mean . . . You mean it was *you* who was selling this?'

'Yeah,' I said. 'That's the old rubbish Alfie Flowers sold me. I'd have never bought it normally, but he caught me when I was a bit *non compos mantis* down at the One Eleven Club. I thought I'd never get shot of it, but you know me, Rodders—he who dares wins! And as it happens, I made a tidy little profit on it as well!'

'But how are we supposed to get rid of it? Mickey thought we'd shift it out of town but even the carrot-crunchers are going to have second thoughts about this lot.'

I gave them Lesson Number One from the Peckham

Business School: 'Why don't you do what I did and find a couple of right berks with cash on the hip?'

Although I had a shrewd suspicion Rodders was feeling the cold wind of recession up his trouser leg, I had a right blinding week. I gave Grandad a punnet of strawberries to celebrate whilst I put the kettle on and settled down with my *FT*.

'You're splashing out a bit, ain't yer?' he opined.

'Grandad,' I said, 'my quarterly figures have shown a sharp upturn. The investors are well chuffed. I even got rid of them technicolour woollen tea cosies I bought.'

'How did you manage that?' he asked with a look of pure forty-two-carrot admiration. 'I mean who the hell wants woollen tea cosies these days?'

'Nobody. I got Mrs Murphy at number nine to sew up all the holes. Then I whipped them down the youth centre and flogged them to the West Indian lads as soppy hats!'

I've always been a great believer in the single most important lesson from the Peckham Business School: operate a high-dividend policy. This seemed as good a time as any to put something aside for the housekeeping and slip Grandad a tenner.

'Don't squander it,' I said.

His eyes gleamed. 'I'll invest it wisely. By the way, how's young Rodney doing?'

Despite appearances, it gave me no pleasure to record the interim results of the Pearce Partnership.

'The opposition is floundering somewhat. Well, to be more precise they're going down like a one-legged man in an hokeycokey. I've seen Rodney a few times this week, skulking around garden centres and what have you.' I stifled a laugh.

'He still ain't got rid of them lawnmower engines?'

I shook my head. 'They're still in their depot— Mickey Pearce's garden shed. Did you know that Tuesday night a burglar broke in and nicked two of them?'

'Oh, no! That's rotten, ain't it! I feel sorry for young Rodney.'

'It's all right, Grandad,' I said. 'Wednesday night he broke in again and put them back!'

I picked up the *FT*, checked out the Don Jones Index and then turned to the telly page. I'm always looking to expand in the entertainment sector. I looked at my watch; 5 p.m. I was toying with the idea of a dawn raid on the video shop when Rodney came in looking like he'd had a poisoned umbrella up the jacksey.

'Long lunch?' I said.

'A bit hefty. With a client . . .'

He flapped across the room. The sole of his shoe looked in need of major collective surgery.

'How are things?' I said.

'Oh, fine.' He sat down at the table. 'Couldn't be better.'

'Good! Got rid of them lawnmower engines yet?'

'Lawnmower engines? Oh, *those* lawnmower engines. Er, not yet. We've had loads of inquiries but we decided to hang out for the right price.'

I nodded. 'That's the best way. *Agent provocateur*, as the French say!'

'Yeah, that's what I thought.'

He picked up a couple of Grandad's strawberries. When they were half-way to his mouth he said: 'That reminds me. Did the paper boy bring my *Sun* this morning?'

I summoned up a look of infinite sadness. 'We had to cancel it, Rodders. You ain't paid your bill.'

He felt in his pockets. 'I've got a bit of a cash-flow problem.'

'How can you have a cash-flow problem, Rodney?' Grandad said. 'I thought you had nearly two hundred pounds left out of your share.'

'That's right. But . . . Mickey's holding the money. Er . . . He's financial director, see . . .'

I'd always thought of Grandad as TITCO's sleeping partner but he was all there that day. 'Why don't you pop round his house and pick it up?'

'He's . . . he's out of town at the moment.'

'I thought I hadn't seen him around for the last four or five days.'

'No, we've been negotiating this *big* deal, and Mickey's gone away to tie up some loose ends.'

'I think he may have shifted your assets offshore, Rodders,' I said. 'I met his mum this morning. She said he sent her a postcard—from Benidorm.'

'*Benidorm?*'

I got the feeling Mickey's trip hadn't been ratified by all the principal shareholders. 'According to the postcard, everything's going well. Food's good, weather's fine. He's met some Swedish girl called Helga. She must be the contact on the deal.'

'What? Oh, yeah, yeah . . .' Rodney looked like he was about to apply for a mail-order course with Exit.

'I admire your bottle, Rodney. I mean, opening a Spanish branch so soon! Not content with cornering the world market in broken lawnmower engines—what are you buying up now, underwater pedalloes?'

'No, um . . . We're going into the self-catering holi-day trade . . .'

'Well, Mickey seems to have catered for himself!'

'We're starting small . . .'

'What you got?' Grandad asked. 'A Wendy House?'

'Look, I can't go into this in any more detail. It's confidential information.'

'I understand, Rodders, I understand!' I said. 'Well, I'm off out. I thought I'd have a couple of tequila sunsets at the Nag's then go on to the Star of Bengal for a Ruby Murray. Coming?'

'Well, I'm potless!'

'Sorry?' I said. 'What did you say?'

'I was just thinking—I suppose I should really stay in and do the company accounts . . .'

Grandad stirred his stumps and picked up the receipt for Lot 37 from off the sideboard. 'Here they are,' he said.

I watched Rodney for a moment, then moved over and put my arm round his shoulder. In body language terms, it was a classic Peckham Business School move. 'Do you honestly think I'm *that* hard?'

He grinned, relieved. 'Nah!'

'Of course I'm not!'

He put his coat on. 'Cheers, Del!'

I turned to Grandad. 'Do him an egg and chips while I'm out, will you? And don't charge him for the chips.'

I caught Young Towser down the Star and decided to trigger phase two of Rodney's further education.

'Sit yourself down and have a popadum,' I said.

'Oi, listen,' he said. 'I can't get involved. I'm getting a take-away for the missus and I promised I'd be back tonight.'

I poured him a glass of wine.

'I'm glad I bumped into you, my son. I want you do to me a favour.'

He didn't look as enthusiastic as you would expect.

'You know them rotten old lawnmower engines that soppy-cods Rodney's been lumbered with? I want you to buy them off him.'

It took Towser a while to catch on. 'Come off it, Del! Alfie Flowers offered me them engines a month ago. I don't want nothing to do with them.'

I brought out my wad and suddenly had his undivided attention. 'I'll give you the money. There you are. Offer him two hundred quid for them.'

'Two hundred! They're only worth about a score in scrap value!'

I smiled my Dave Trump smile. 'The art of the deal, my son,' I said.

Towser looked none the wiser.

'I want him to think he's made a good profit. Look, he's had a bad week. He's been tucked up something chronic by his best friend and now he's brassic.'

'Why don't you just give him the money?'

''Cos it'll seem like charity.'

'And he'll be too proud to accept it?'

'Oh, no,' I said. 'He'd snap it up like

When outing the merchandise, make sure you're on to a royalty. Prince Charles is the best, but one of the others will do.

a shot! It's just that I want him to believe he's succeeded for once. I also want him to think he's proved me wrong. It's important, Towser.'

'All right, Del, if that's what you want . . .'

'You're a pal. And don't let him know that I'm behind all this. Tell him . . . Er, tell him you've got a contact in the Parks Department at the GLC, he can't get enough lawnmower engines, that sort of thing. See, I won't be losing on the deal, 'cos by this time tomorrow Rodney'll want to be my partner again, so he'll have to give me that money back.'

I sat back, well chuffed. But Towser was way behind. In the John Harvey-Oswald stakes he would have been a non-starter.

'Wait a minute,' he said. 'What am I supposed to do with these engines?'

'Dump them somewhere!'

'I can't do that, Del. I got nicked for fly-dumping a few months back. They'd chuck the book at me this time!'

'Well, take them back to Alfie Flowers and tell him he can have them for nothing.'

'All right, Del. Here, what's in it for me?'

I sighed and put three fivers next to the remains of my prawn vindaloo. You've got to hand it to Towser. Or he'll take it.

He folded his arms.

'Twenty?' I said.

'Anything for a mate!'

I left him with the rest of his wine. I don't know how long it took him to notice I'd also left him with the bill.

Rodney was taking the weight off his brain at the

Nag's the next afternoon. He still hadn't fixed his rhythm and blues. He probably hadn't factored a visit to the cobbler into his schedule.

'All right, Rodders?' I greeted him. 'I've had a good day, my son! Here, there was a silly bloke down the market, must have come from one of them homes. I asked him if he fancied buying a load of old lawn-mower engines—but he said he weren't *that* silly!'

'For your information, Derek,' he announced, 'this morning I successfully negotiated the sale of those engines to Young Towser!'

'You're kidding me!'

'On my life! He bought the lot. He's got a contact in the Parks Department of the GLC.'

'Well, that's a stroke of luck ain't it!'

'It's got nothing to do with luck, Del. It's good business. I knew all along that if I held on long enough, I'd get my price.'

'Well, I've got to hand it to you, Rodney. It must have taken courage.'

'He who dares wins, eh, Del?'

'That's right! Well, Mickey'll be pleased when he gets back, won't he?'

Rodney frowned. 'Don't talk to me about Mickey. I've liquidated the partnership.'

'I'm very sorry to hear that, Rodders,' I said. 'Still, sooner or later every financial wizard has got to try going it alone, it's *oeuf sur le plat . . .*'

'Well . . . I was thinking . . . Well, you know . . .'

I smiled. 'Go back to how it was, shall we? You and me?'

'Yeah! You and me, Del! And now I've got experience of buying and selling . . .'

'That could be invaluable, Rodney. Right then, let's not hang around. Let's pool our resources. How much did you sell them engines for?'

'Two—er, one hundred and sixty-five pounds.'

I thought it was time for a swift audit. 'You *sure* that's all you got, Rodney?'

He didn't turn a hair. 'That's not bad, Del. I mean they were only worth a score in scrap value!'

'You certainly have learnt a lot, Rodders. Let's see the colour of your money then.'

'Oh, I haven't got the money.'

'Didn't Towser pay you?'

'Oh, yeah, he paid me. I've invested it all.'

'You've done *what*?' A sixth sense told me that Rodney wasn't the only one that was going to learn a lesson.

'Well, you said a trader's only as good as his stock, so I went down Alfie Flowers' yard and got us another load of lawnmower engines!'

I experienced a sharp pain in the wallet. 'No, Rodney,' I croaked. 'Tell me it's a joke.'

'Towser said his man at the GLC can't get enough of those engines! I was dead lucky down at

Alfie's. He'd just had another load delivered this morning. Don't worry, Del, they're the same as the first lot!'

'You bet your bloody life they're the same! What a forty-two-carrot plonker you are!'

'Hey, come on, Del, don't you think it's time you showed a bit of faith in me?'

'Yeah, yeah, whatever you want, Rodney,' I muttered. Not for the first time, I set about revising TITCO's profit forecast.

Rodney was silent for a moment, but I knew it couldn't last.

'Del, I was wondering. Seeing as we're partners again, do you reckon you could help me out? I mean, I ain't had a pint all week, I've only eaten Grandad's cooking and the sole's coming off my best plimsoles . . .'

I managed a smile as I brought out what was left of my wad. 'Yeah, I'll help you out, Rodney,' I said. I took the rubber band off and handed it to him. 'Wrap that round your foot, that'll keep your sole on.'

CHAPTER TWO

....

There's No Such Thing as Luck

If there's one thing I've learnt from my struggle to reach the top, it's this: you don't win the raffle if you ain't bought a ticket. And another thing: make sure your ticket is the first one out the drum.

Take the great entrepruners—Richard Branston, Sir John Harvey-Oswald, Ali Fayed. They weren't just touched by the hand of fate. They didn't wake up one morning, take a sniff of the Bostik and nip off to buy Harrods. Good fortune didn't simply fall off the back of a lorry and into their grateful mitts.

Granted, if you turned Rodney's luck into a film, it'd be the biggest tear-jerker since *Love Story*, but don't get fogged off with all that old fanny about destiny. You can make your own luck, and I'm going to show you how.

Rodders and I were down the Nag's not so long ago, pondering a sharp downturn on one or two new business initiatives. Our exclusive range of Yves Saint Dior parfums, hand-bottled by Rodney, had just gone down the toilette. So had our genuine mink coats.

Ethiopian mink too, at only fifty quid a shot. They was a little on the tabby side, as mink goes, but as long as the punters didn't have a dog they'd have been purring.

'I thought we'd have a right result with this scent, Rodders,' I said. 'I thought they'd be queueing up for it—camp beds on the pavement. Instead . . .' I pulled an imaginary khazi chain.

'We did sell one bottle, Del,' Rodney said, 'but she fetched it back. Said the last time she smelt an odour like that was when the cat sanctuary got bombed during the war.'

Marque de fabrique, I thought. That was hardly what you might call economies of scale. But I wasn't dented. Win some, lose some, that's what we say at the Peckham Business School.

I said it again after losing three nights on the trot at Boycie's poker table. I'd taken Mum's lucky rabbit foot with me as well. Brought me about as much luck as it did the rabbit.

'A losing streak is like joining the Moonies,' Trig observed helpfully during an emergency AGM at the bar afterwards. 'Easy to get into but a bark to get out of.'

Rodney seized the chance to give me some grief about gambling away the partnership profits, but I was more than ready for him. He who anticipates wins.

'You don't know nothing about cards, Rodney,' I told him. 'You and your little friends are still playing strip snap, ain't you?' I leaned across to Trig. 'I hear they're thinking of asking some girls along one day.'

I've always been a great believer in the Peckham Business School's most basic lesson: the harder you duck and dive, the luckier you get. Though there are some days when you chuck a fiver in the air and it comes down a summons.

Rodney was normally a great one for mixing business with pleasure, but that little jest went down about as well as a poll-tax bill. 'How much we got left, Del?' he asked, menacingly.'

'You got a hankie handy? I didn't want you worrying. I couldn't stand all that dermatitis again.'

'How much?'

'Seventy quid.'

He blew a sigh of relief. 'Well, at least we can put the central heating back on and get something to eat.'

'I'm not wasting it on food and warmth,' I said. 'This is my stake money for tonight's game.'

Rodney's reply will not be recorded by posterity, because who should come in at this point but Boycie, all smiles in his wide-awake suit and nine-carrot tom.

'What's up with you, Rodney?' he said. 'Bird

trouble? You look like you've had a promise from a liar. How's your luck, Del?'

I looked Peckham's answer to John De Lorry straight in the eye.

'Changing fast, pal. We've just outed two hundred and fifty quid's worth of French scent this morning.'

Boycie guffawed. 'Good, so you're in the chair, are you? I'll have a cognac. Better make it a small one though. Don't want to skint you before tonight's game.'

No way was I taking this slur upon our solvency lying down.

'Betty!' I said, 'Give us a cognac—and make it a *double*.' There's no place for midgets in the modern business world. You've got to think big, brave and brazen. 'And I'll have a large—a *large*—Chivas Regal *with* coke.'

That showed him.

Rodney ordered a double Southern Comfort with American dry.

'And half of lager for Rodney,' I said. I didn't want to overdo it.

I handed Betty a ten-pound note and delivered my *coup de resistance*.

'Have one yourself,' I said. 'And put the change in the Third World relief bottle!'

I turned to Boycie. 'So how's business, pal?'

'Not too good. I've sold one today, a 1980 Simca

26

Estate. Only made eight hundred and fifty out of it. I mean, what's eight hundred and fifty these days? It don't heat my swimming-pool for a week.'

'Grim, ain't it?' Rodney commensurated.

'Right. So I said to Marlene, if it wasn't for the fact that I'm winning so much off Del and the boys, we'd have to do something drastic—like only have smoked salmon *twice* a week.'

'You've got more front than Brighton, ain't you?' I said. 'I've told you, Boycie, my luck's changing. I'm on a winning streak.'

Boycie gave me the sort of smile that makes him look like a constipated rat. Little did he realize what the maestro had in store for him. I slapped a twenty-quid note on the counter.

'There's a score that says the next customer in orders a pint of something.'

'You're on!' he said. 'Twenty says the next customer orders a short.'

Rodney grabbed me by the arm. 'You're pushing your luck a bit, Del!'

'Don't worry, Rodders,' I said out the corner of my mouth, 'I've seen the next customer come past the window.'

I had too. The pub doors swung open and in came a party-size Irish navvy, all mud and donkey jacket.

I gave the profit-and-loss a mental once-over. I was a tenner down after buying the drinks, but Boycie's twenty would put me back ten ahead. I was well pleased. I was just reaching for the readies when the Paddy opened his mouth.

'I'll have a dry Martini and a slimline tonic,' he said.

Coq au vin! I'd put twenty quid on a MacAlpine's navvy on a diet. What's the odds on you backing the only Provo weightwatcher in London?

'Don't worry about it,' I told Rodders when Boycie had gone.

'Why can't you just tell Boycie the game's off?' Rodney asked. 'Say you've caught something.'

I felt it was time to give him a slice of Lee Hokeycokey.

'Rodney, let me explain something to you. Beneath all this finery,' I rattled my medallions, 'there lies . . . a berk. That suprises you, don't it?'

He was too flabbergasted to respond.

'See, the day Dad left home—Mum hadn't been gone very long—you were just a little nipper with a pink patch on your National Health specs to help your lazy eye. Grandad was sitting in his armchair waiting for colour television to be invented. I came home that evening and found that Dad had taken his things and left us. He didn't just take *his* things, he took everything, except the money Mum had left me and you—and that was only because I'd hid it too well.

'He'd left us with nothing, not even the price of a meal. And d'you know what that day was? It was my sixteenth birthday. He even took my cake!

'I swore to myself then that no matter what happened in my life I would never run away. And that's why I'm a berk. It's people like me who wrestle with wild animals! That's why I've got to play tonight's game, because I *can't* run away. D'you understand me?'

When I'd finished, I think I saw tears in his eyes. 'Yeah I understand you, Del,' he said. 'And I'll tell you what, Del, we're going to beat Boycie tonight!'

It must have been a lot like this at Dunkirk. 'That's the spirit, Rodders,' I said. 'We'll take him to the cleaners.'

'They'll call our flat Chez Sketchley by the time we've finished! I'll see you later Del. I'm going to get you some stake money.'

This was a turn-up. 'Where from?'

'When the chips are down I can be as sharp as you, Del. Do you remember that party we had at the flat last month? There was plenty to drink, weren't there?'

In the adventure capital game, you've got to put your accessories where your mouth is.

'You're going to organize a disco?'

'No. I'm going to take the empties back for you!'

Sometimes, even the Peckham Business School ain't got the know-how to deal with Rodney. You live with someone for all these years and you think you really understand them. Then something like this happens— a simple gesture—and you suddenly realize what a one hundred per cent, twenty-four-carrot plonker they've turned into.

Boycie came round that night in his beige three-piece, carrying a briefcase. Even Trig had made an effort to smarten himself up. I must have told him once about the importance of psyching up the opposition. He pulled out his piggy bank and emptied a small bundle of crumpled notes on to the table.

Me, I pulled out a century. You've got to lead from the front.

'Is that all you've got, Del?' Boycie sneered. He opened his case and pulled out three thick wads. There must have been a thousand quid there.

'No,' I said hastily. 'Rodney's looking after the rest.'

Rodney took this as his cue. Defiance burning in his eyes, he dropped a five-pound note on to the baize.

'There's the four pounds thirty-seven from the emp-ties, Del Boy,' he said. 'I bankrolled the rest.'

I closed my eyes and thought of Mum's grave. I

wondered if there was room in it for any other members of the family.

The game got too heavy for Trig very early on.

The thing about Trig is, he don't grasp that we all go through bad patches. I've felt a bit gutty myself on occasion. But what separates the wheat from the chaffinches is how we react. There are those who are knocked down and just stay there. And there are those who pick themselves up, dust themselves down and start all over again. Trig didn't graduate from that school. In fact, he didn't go to school at all. His Dad died a couple of years before he was born and where it says Father's Name on his birth certificate his Mum wrote: 'Some soldiers'.

'It's just you and me then, Del,' Boycie said.

I'm sure I detected a note of fear in his voice. Either that, or the smoke from Rodney's and Grandad's roll-ups was getting to him.

'Thirty quid if you want to stay in.'

I'd only got thirty quid left. I looked at him through narrowed eyes and lit a Castella. 'I'll see you.'

Boycie fanned out his cards. *Place de la Concord!* A running flush—four, five, six, seven and eight of hearts.

'Je . . .' I said. 'I've only got three tens.'

Boycie's smile reminded me of a bulldog chewing a wasp.

But I wasn't finished yet. I pulled out another wad of notes. It was the money that Mum left us. I swore to her I'd only use it in a life-or-death situation, and this was it. This was no longer a game—this was a duel, the kind of eyeball-to-eyeball encounter fought out every day in the boardrooms of the rich and famous.

'I've got five hundred quid here that says the game ain't over . . .'

Boycie was impressed. 'Nice one, Del Boy, I like your style. Let's make it a bit exciting, shall we? No limit!'

That suited me. Suited me right down to the ground. This was like the battle for Distillers. One day they'd reconstruct this game on *News at Ten*.

We played another hand and Boycie kicked off with a hundred. I saw him and raised him a hundred.

'You're bluffing,' I said.

'Only one way to find out, ain't there?'

He *was* bluffing. I could tell by his eyes, he was definitely bluffing.

'Trust me, Rodney, trust me—he's bluffing!' I said. 'I've got him by the short and curlies.'

This wasn't gambling, this was business.

'Your hundred,' I said. 'And another two hundred. Do you want to see me, Boycie?'

I had him on the ropes.

'Oh, no, my old mate. Your two hundred—and I'll raise you a grand!'

The room went quiet.

'Play the game, son,' Grandad said to Boycie. 'That's the money their Mum left them. That's all they've got!'

Boycie was unmoved. 'Well, Del, do something or get off the pot.'

Like a red rag to a bull, that was. I pulled off my jewellery and looked around for other investors. Rodney and Grandad were looking everywhere round the room except at me. Somehow I didn't think they were ever going to make it as adventure capitalists. I looked at Trig. He looked at me, then tossed his car keys on the table.

'Cheers, Trig, you're a pal. Trigger's car, Boycie— it's a good one!'

'You must be joking. I sold it to him!'

Trade or stay poor. He who dares wins. In the business jungle, when the going gets tough, the tough get their gongs off. It was a big moment. In my mind's eye, women screamed and strong men wept openly as I unfastened my medallion.

'Right—my jewellery, Trig's car and everything in the flat. The stereos, the tellies, the fridge, the cooker, the deep freeze, the beds and wardrobes, our clothes . . .'

'What the bloody hell d'you think you're playing at?' was all I got from Rodney. I realized then how important it is for generals to get proper support from their privates.

'He's bluffing, Rodney—I've got him beat! Have faith, Rodders.'

I think Boycie knew he'd met his match. He agreed to let me see him.

'I've got kings,' he said.

'How many?' I asked, fighting the slight involuntary movement of my Adam's apple brought on by the whiff of success.

Boycie laid his cards, one at a time, on the table.

'*Un—deux—trois—quatre.*'

Ordre du jour! You don't have to be Chas Aznavour to know what that's the French for.

'Four!' I couldn't believe it.

'I didn't know you were good at maths, Del.'

'I thought you were bluffing.'

'What did you have, Del?' Trig asked, eager to wash our dirty corporate linen in public.

I hesitated. 'Two pairs.'

'Two pairs?' groaned Grandad. 'You went all that way on two rotten pairs?'

'I thought he was bluffing.' I knew my face was the picture of abject defeat.

'Couldn't give us a lift home, could you?' Trig asked.

Boycie leered. 'I'll send the boys round to pick up the stuff tomorrow. It pains me, Del, it really pains me.'

If you'd asked me at that moment what was the sweetest sound in the world, I'd have been torn between saying the crisp crinkle of Boycie's thousand

34

freshly minted smackeroonyos in my pocket or the dull thud of his body hitting the lino.

Boycie stretched out to scoop up the winnings.

I grabbed his wrist.

'You know the rules of the game, Boycie. All cards must be seen before winnings can be collected.'

'Leave it out, will you, Del?' Trig said. 'You've only got two pairs.'

'No, no, Trig. Let him have his little moment. Let's see your two pairs, Del.'

So I showed him. I showed them all. I laid my first pair on the table.

'I've got one pair of aces.'

Then I laid another pair on the table.

'And I've got another pair of aces.'

Chambourcy nouvelle! If you could have seen Boycie's face!

'Where d'you get them from?' he hissed in my ear.

'Same place you got them four kings,' I said. 'I knew you were cheating, Boycie.'

'How?'

''Cos that weren't the hand I dealt you!'

CHAPTER THREE

Looking the Part

Image—that's what the financial world is all about. The right appearance can fool the customer every time. Take me, for instance. I'm a perfect example. I look exactly what I am, but that's only 'cos I know how to give the right image.

It's the little things. The watch, the tie pin, the chunky identity bracelet. The rollneck and sheepskin, the camelhair and kipper tie. The Mercedes key ring, the Filofax. When people see me with these they know exactly what I am. It's better than a mason's handshake.

Rodney used to say: 'Del thinks all you need is a Filofax and a pair of red braces and you're chairman of the board.' Trust Rodney to get it wrong. That ain't the half of it. You can't afford to skimp on the accessories. You need a trendy green trenchcoat, an Arnie Becker aluminium executive briefcase and a small tortoiseshell cigar holder too.

I dread to think how Rodders will cut the mustard now he's said *bonjour* to the family seat and got hitched to Cassandra. I mean, show Rodders a Peckham Business School sandwich course and most of it would end up on his lapel—and that don't look too clever when you're stronging it with the top Two Hundred.

Let's face it, whether you're in the boardroom or the billiard room, clothes maketh the mogul. I'll give you a for instance. When

Us yuppies love a bit of Berlin wall on the mantelpiece. I get all mine hand-sprayed down the builder's yard in Herrington Road.

Rodney met that Lady Victoria Marsham Hales down the market, he'd have been in dead stuke if I hadn't steered him through a couple of major social minefields.

I didn't notice her at first. I was busy giving a client a lesson in style. I was outing thirty-six-piece canteens of hand-made Indonesian cutlery for three pounds fifty.

'See that price tag?' I said. 'It says: "Manufacturer's recomended retail price, forty-two pounds, ninety-nine pence".'

He said I could have printed them myself.

'Do me a favour, pal,' I said. 'Do I look like Rupert Maxwell?'

'There are two Ms in recommended.'

'That's the Indonesian spelling, you berk!'

38

But he wouldn't leave it alone. 'They can't be quality; they're too cheap!'

I shook my head. Even the Peckham Business School would have a tough time sorting out this berk.

'How can anything be *too* cheap, you plonker?'

'Listen,' he said. 'I'm not a plonker!'

'So what are you doing?' I asked. 'An impression?'

Making an impression. That's what this chapter of *The Trotter Way to Millions* is all about.

Lady Victoria made one on Rodney when she showed him the XJS her dad gave her as a birthday present, and she made one on me when Rodders showed me a picture of her and Princess Anne in *Country Life*.

At first I thought he'd got Berk's Peerage out of the library to look up some of his old college mates, but then I realized he was mugging up on the heraldic and gynaecological history of the nobility. I've always felt at home with the nobs, so I asked him to give me the SP.

'Vicky's old man's very wealthy,' he said. 'Have you ever heard of the Duke of Maylebury?'

'Bloody hell!' I said. 'Albert, that little sort Rodney's with—her father owns a pub!'

It turned out he also owned Handsome Samson, the second favourite for the next year's Derby, and he was a peer of the realm and all. Sir Henry Marsham,

KGB, GLC, BO and Bar! He even had a country gaff. To a major-league player like myself, it was just like coming home.

Fair enough, I thought. Rodney has a lot of qualities. She might have been smitten by his rakish charm and boyish good looks. Then again she could have been a posh tart who fancied a bit of scrag. Either way, I was going to have to show him a bit of *je ne sais pas pourquoi*.

'Me and Vicky have got a lot in common,' Rodders said.

I couldn't help thinking she had a lot and he was just common.

I started putting together a business plan later that day. Rodney was taking the weight off his Doc Martens in the TITCO executive dining-room and sucking on a roll-up.

'You know,' I said, 'when the Duke says *bonjour* to this mortal curl, Vicky'll become a Duchess.' I nodded at Rodney. 'I want you to remember this moment, Albert. We could be looking at the future Duke of Maylebury! Give him a cornet, a bit of vermin, get rid of them boots . . .'

I managed to cop four tickets to the opera. Rodney liberated his evening suit from the pawn shop and I liberated June from Zimbabwe House for a joint cultural encounter. I've always been *au fate* with gracious living.

'Figaro, Figaro, Figaro,' I hummed as we made our way to our seats. Carmen's always been one of my favourites. I could see Vicky was dead impressed.

Everyone there was rattling their tomfoolery like it was going out of style. Lovely jubbly! This was my kind of gaff. I decided to make an evening of it. I went and got some bacon-flavoured crisps, dry-roasted peanuts and choc ices half-way through the first number.

When Vicky and Rodney left at the interval, I was forced to admit that things hadn't gone all our way. Then again, perhaps it was just as well.

'I'm sorry about tonight, Del Boy,' June said as we strolled back to the van. 'I don't know what came over me!'

'Nor did that woman in front of you!' I said. I thought June might have overdone it with the Benedictines and lemonades, the fizzy orange juice, the crisps, the peanuts, the liquorice allsorts and the choc ices.

'Before I came out I had a blancmange,' she said. 'The milk must have been off.'

Unfortunately, she had another psychedelic yodel

Image is all about being in the right place at the right time with the right accessories. It ain't just a question of nine-to-five, Mondays to Fridays. Not by a long chalk.

41

in the van, but you could hardly notice as we motored into town the next day—especially if you stuck your head out the window.

I parked my thoroughbred amongst three-wheelers outside a gents' outfitters in South Moulton Street and tasked them with the challenge of turning Rodney into Nigel Ravers for the weekend.

'I thought you meant we'd pop down to Solbros in Balham for an hairy shirt or something,' he complained as I pointed out a couple of Barbers. 'I didn't realize I'd have to dress up like a free-range wally!'

'But this ain't just any weekend, is it?' I explained patiently. 'It's a weekend with the aristocracy. Earls, barons, Royals, the lot. You can't go to Covington House decked out as a Bob Geldof lookalike!'

'A pair of green wellies ain't going to turn me into the Archduke Ferdinand,' he said.

As the manager approached, I knew that I was back in the driving seat.

'What is sir's pleasure?' He looked like he'd just copped the rest of June's blancmange. I glanced at the shoulder of my best camelhair.

'Well, birds and curry, I suppose,' I said, putting him at his ease. 'But I didn't come here for chit chat. I want you to tog my brother out for a weekend in the country. Hacking jacket, stout brogues and all the Xs. A monkey should cover it.' I slapped my wad on the counter.

'Don't you worry, Rodney,' Albert said. 'By the time he's finished with you, you'll look just like one of them.'

Rodders wasn't totally sold on the idea. 'That's what I'm afraid of,' he said.

Me and Albert thought it best to go and keep an eye on Rodders whilst he put his plus fives and hipflask through their paces amongst the carrot-crunchers.

We didn't actually have an invite, but as I gunned the Reliant through the field towards the shoot, I could see they was well pleased to see us. Rodders let both barrels off into the air as a welcome. Sir Henry legged it over to greet me as I slotted the van in between two Range Rovers.

'Tally-ho!' I said. I took a deep breath. Wet tweeds and cordite. It was my kind of party.

Vicky made the introductions.

'I've seen your boat race in *The Sporting Life*,' I said to Sir Henry. 'How is Handsome Samson? Over that fetlock sprain? I hope he'll be trying come the Derby!'

I could see I'd made an impression. I reached into my camelhair and brought out a Castella. 'Your Grace,' I said, 'would you mind awfully if I had a little pot-shot before tea?'

Sir Henry was open-mouthed with admiration. He waved his butler over to supply me with a shooter.

I gave him my Clint Eastwood smile. 'That's

perfectly all right. I have my own weapon. Albert, my man, would you mind?'

The old sea dog went muttering to the van.

'He's been with us for years,' I said. 'Like income tax.' You've got to talk to people in a language they understand.

I sighted my gun and called to the clay-pigeon loader. 'Ready when you are, John!'

'I think you mean Paul!' he shouted back.

'Sorry, Paul,' I said. 'In your own time, my son.'

I blew away both pigeons with the one shot, then rested the gun on my hip as I took another drag on my Castella. 'What-ho, your Worship,' I said. 'These sawn-off, pump-action jobs certainly do the business, eh?'

'Where did you get that from?' Rodney whispered in admiration.

'I borrowed it off Iggy Higgins.'

'Iggy Higgins? But Iggy Higgins *robs banks*!'

'I know,' I said. 'But it's Saturday!'

Rodney was even more nervous than usual when we got changed into our evening suits. I realized I was going to have to show him a bit more than which hand he held his knife and fork in.

As we went downstairs there was dowagers wall to wall. 'This is the *crème de la menthe* of British nobility,' I said. 'We don't want them thinking we're the oi

polloi or something, so we've got to be on our bestest behaviour.'

A bird in a low-cut dress crossed the hall below us and I had to reach for my first half of sherry. 'Cor,' I said. 'Look at the lungs on that.'

I found the Duke in a corridor full of Old Masters.

'All right, Henry?'

'Good evening, Trotter,' he said.

I gave the painting behind him the once-over. 'Is that a da Vinci?'

'It is not.'

'Shame,' I said. 'He's my favourite. He did the Mona Lisa and all.'

This was news to him. 'Did he really?'

I nodded. 'Her with the energetic smile. You can't tell whether she's grinning or sucking a bull's-eye.'

'That's a Pissarro.' He sounded a bit choked.

A half sovereign ring says a lot about a man. Combined with a medallion, it speaks volumes.

'I don't know,' I said reassuringly. 'I've seen worse!'

'Dear God! It's a Camille Pissarro. He was a nineteenth-century Impressionist.'

'Get away,' I said. 'Like Mike Yarwood?'

Dinner with the aristocracy was a blinder. In fact,

with Patterson (Sir Henry's ancient container) giving me a regular topperooni every time he went by, there was some bits Rodney had to remind me about afterwards.

I do remember giving the dowager on my right the lowdown about Rodders' forthcoming engagement to Vicky.

'*Engaged!*' The old duck was really excited.

'Keep it under your tiara,' I said. 'We don't want the media getting hold of this. You know what it was like for Andrew and Fergie—couldn't fart without a newsflash, could they?'

Patterson plonked a decanter of port in front of me. I took a swig and decided it was as good a time as any to show Sir Henry a thing or two about breeding. I licked my finger and ran it round the rim of the Dowager's goblet. Magic! It went off like an air-raid siren.

'That's how you can tell they're pukka crystal.'

'Really?' he said. 'Thank you.'

I was on a roll. It was just like giving a seminar at the Peckham Business School. I lobbed my banana skin into one of them Ming dustbins and picked up a fruit knife.

'Henry,' I said. 'This knife . . .'

'No,' he said. 'It's not a da Vinci.'

'Pure silver all the same, I'd wager.'

46

'Yes,' he said. 'They were made by William Cawdill in 1648.'

'Really?' I turned it towards the light. 'They've come up well, ain't they?'

I downed the other half of the decanter and promised them all a butcher's at one or two bargains on the cutlery front that I'd brought up in the van. But first I had to clear up the little matter of Rodders' criminal record. 'I want you all to know,' I said, 'in case the drugs conviction is ever brought up by the gutter press, he was done up like a kipper!'

In sophisticated company these things are always better out in the open. All the same, this lot still looked a bit down in the mouth, so I gave them the first couple of verses of 'Don't worry, Mother, your son will soon be back; he's only sailing round the world in a Grimsby fishing smack'.

Henry invited me to join him in his study for the encore. Rodders looked very disappointed, so I reckoned I'd cheer him up by having a word in mine host's earhole about the wedding.

I sat down behind the desk and helped myself to a Castella the size of a salami, then took another for later.

'You know, Henry,' I said, 'there's a rumour we're related to the Surrey Trotters!'

It's funny how people can change when you're

alone with them. He went very red and started to foam at the mouth.

'I don't care if you're related to the Berkshire Trotters, the Pig's Trotters or the Harlem Bloody Globe Trotters!' he bellowed. 'I want your brother out of my daughter's life!'

I sat back in my chair and gave some to the Castella. Call it instinct, call it a lifetime at the PBS, but I knew it was time to get down to business.

'*You* certainly made an impression, Del,' Rodney said when we found ourselves back at Trotter Tower the next morning.

I thought I probably had. I'd woken up feeling like someone had put a hamster in my mouth.

'It was the sort of impression the Yanks made on Nagasaky!' he said. 'But do you know the most painful incident of the entire evening? It wasn't you telling the joke about the Irish bloke on a skiing holiday. It wasn't even what you did in that punch bowl. It was when the Duke told me he wanted me out of Vicky's life for good . . .' He paused. 'Del, he even offered me *money*!'

'*No!*' I said.

'Yeah. You can imagine how I felt.'

'Horrible, Rodney, horrible. I'd have told him what to do with his money.'

'I did,' Rodney said.

'*What?*' I said, '*You said nito to a grand?*'

'Yes, I did! I still had a little bit of my self-esteem left intact. A thousand pounds don't buy me, Del.'

'Well, it could buy me!' I said.

'A free estimate could buy you.' His eyes seemed to get closer together. 'How did you know he offered me a grand?'

'Well,' I said reasonably, 'that's about the going rate for getting a plonker out of your daughter's life!'

'You arranged it, didn't you?'

I nodded. 'But you turned it down, you dipstick.'

'Yes, I did!' he said, then smiled. 'I said make it twelve hundred and you've got a deal.'

CHAPTER FOUR

The Good News Bible

At the conclusion of a particularly audacious piece of business I'm often asked where I get my inspiration from. Whether

It is never easy in the entreprunerial game. If the Driscoll Brothers don't get you, a computer virus will.

it's selling Nelson's eye-patches to the tourists in Trafalgar Square, taking on a shipment of Borneo-manufactured cordless phones or investing in a consignment of fire-damaged woks, the question on most punters' lips is: 'Del Boy, how did you spot the SP on this when it looked to me like a load of old cobblers?'

My answer is simple. I owe my uncanny business instincts and fiscal genius to the Great Dealmaker in the Sky, and I'm not talking about Bobby Murdoch. Like Cliff Richards, Lew Grade and all them Maharajas with long hair and fleets of Rollers, I believe God'll Fix It. And, what's more, I believe that even when that tart Rodney drops a major gooley that virtually skints the Trotter empire and casts us out into the financial wilderness, He will show us the way to an earner.

I'll give you a couple of for instances.

It wasn't long ago that the Trotter Path to Success was jammed up worse than the M25. The man from the council had spake unto me and asked whither I had deposited the last three months' rent. There came to pass a great deal of frost and sleet when all TITCO had in stock was summer dresses. We hadn't had a decent miracle since Uncle Albert threw himself down the Nag's Head cellar to try and begat some insurance money. And, lo, executive stress was taking its inevitable toll upon my physical wellbeing. As on many other occasions, I looked up and asked for a sign.

"Ere, Del,' Rodney said as I was anointing myself with Brut to greet the new day. 'When you're in the khazi do you ever get the feeling that you're . . . well, not alone?'

'No,' I said. 'Why, do you?'

'No, no . . . It's just that Albert reckons it's possessed.'

'Possessed? Do me a favour. Give it a couple of months and it might be re-possessed!'

'Elsie Partridge reckons it's haunted,' Albert said. Elsie was the first old bird he'd found in a while who didn't fly away when he started talking about how he sank the *Bismarck*.

I was laughing so hard I had to put a spoonful of Andrews into my brandy.

'Elsie Partridge is a medium!' he said.

I whipped one of the summer dresses off the rack and chucked it across to him. 'Get that round to her. Should fit her a treat!'

'I'm not talking about her dress size—I mean she's a spiritualist. She can contact the departed.'

'No kidding?' I said. 'I bet that's where she pulled you!'

'She has powers, Del. She is one of the true communicators. Back in the early sixties she used to hold regular meetings in that hall above John Collier's. They used to come from miles around to listen to Elsie. They paid thousands of pounds to use her gift.'

For once, Rodney spoke for both of us. 'I think there is more to this occult lark than meets the eye, Del.'

The old Trotter mental software started to hum. I went and sat by Albert.

'You said they paid Elsie Partridge *thousands* of pounds?'

'Yeah,' he said. 'But she never took a penny of it, used to send it all to Battersea Dogs Home. I bet she wished she'd have kept some now. She's only got her pension to live on.'

'But they still paid her all that lovely money!'

'Yeah, people'll pay a fortune to talk to their . . .'

He paused and narrowed his eyes at me. 'No, son, she's retired now.'

I didn't push it. 'Perhaps she'd like a part-time job,' I said.

'Just drop it, eh?' my financial adviser said. That proved it. I was on to something.

'Don't you see what this means?' I said to Albert. 'You told me something would turn up out of the blue to save our bacon. This is it. Me and Elsie Partridge—what a combination. An old age pensioner with a priceless gift and a successful yuppy who's brassic lint! We could make each other rich. I honestly think that God is giving me a sign!'

I looked up to heaven, my boat race a picture of piety. If I'd worn a syrup, I would have been a dead spit for Charlton Heston.

Suddenly I got a pain in my gut that was worse than one of Rodney's ideas. I thought I was having a connery. There was only one thing for it. A couple of Pina Coladas with ice.

Once I'd recovered, I went down the Nag's to sort out a venue for Elsie's séance with Mike. A week later we was in business. All the lads were there. But before too long I felt as welcome as Tiny Mowland does at Harrods.

'You don't honestly believe all that mumbo-jumbo, do you, Michael?' Boycie said. He'd stopped believing in miracles since the doctors told him Marlene couldn't

54

have a child 'cos he was firing more blanks than the Territorials.

'I don't actually *believe* it,' Mike said. 'I just don't like taking the chance.'

Boycie guffawed. He's the only person I know who can do that. 'Del, if Elsie Partridge could really raise the dead, half the money-lenders in Peckham would be employing her. It's a load of old tosh. Only a simpleton would believe in it.'

If God hadn't intended us to be millionaires, why did he give us Concorde, mobile phones and cocktail cabinets in Aston Martins?

'I believe in it,' Trigger said.

'Say no more. You still leave biscuits and a glass of milk out on Christmas Eve.'

Nerys, the barmaid, leapt to my support. 'My mum went to a séance once. She got a message from the other side. It said she would meet a tall bald man who would alter her fortunes.'

'There you are,' I said. 'Lovely jubbly.'

'A week later she got mugged by a skinhead.'

The only way to follow that was to order another Pina Colada. 'And the usual for everyone else, Nerys.'

Mike pulled me to one side. 'Are you paying for these drinks or what, Del?' he said. 'This slate of yours is getting out of hand. That Mrs Partridge has just arrived. She's had food and drink on it . . .'

I knew I had to boost market confidence. 'Don't worry about it, Mike,' I said.

'Over the last month you've had more cocktails than James Bond *and* a fried lunch every day, all on the slate!'

'Give me a couple of weeks, Mike, and I'll sort it out with you . . .'

'You've had about ten packs of cigars on the slate. Even the rent for the upstairs room's on the slate!'

Pas de Calais! I'd offered him a way of re-scheduling the debt, and he was treating me like General Beluga! I had no choice but to give him a glimpse of the Peckham Business School magic.

'Unless your attitude changes, Michael, I may have to consider taking my business elsewhere.' I sat him down. 'Look, just recently I have been sailing the good ship *Trotter* through a little patch of fiscal turbulence. But once I get Elsie Partridge firing on all cylinders I'll be laughing. A month from now she'll be bringing them back to order. I've even got the price list worked out.

'This time next year, Mike, I'll be a millionaire— and think what that'll mean for you. They'll be flocking in here from all corners of the kingdom. So not only will you be getting the rent for the upstairs room,

but when the show's finished all the pilgrims'll be down here having a jolly-up, won't they! Your takings'll treble overnight! You know it makes sense!'

He had that expression he wears when he's halfway through the *Sun* crossword. Finally, he spoke: 'Yeah, I suppose so. I'm still worried, though. We're dealing with the forces of darkness here. I mean, are we going to end up with the table and chairs flying round the bar?'

I gave him my word. 'No more than any other Friday night.'

At that point Elsie ushered us upstairs.

There was me, Rodney, Boycie, Albert, Mike and Trigger sitting round a table. It was better than being in church.

'Remember, Else,' I told her, 'this is just a dummy run. The real séance—when the punters come in with the serious doh-ray-me—is next Tuesday night.'

'Derek,' she said, 'God gave me the gift to communicate with those in the next world. I've never profited from it. I only want to share it with people.'

'And God gave me the gift of making bunce, and I only want to share it with you,' I assured her. 'You're not going to run away from some cash in the pinny, are you?'

She blushed. 'I suppose not . . .'

'So everyone's a winner!' I rubbed my hands.

'Lovely jubbly! Right, ready when you are, Elsie. Eyes down for a full house. We're off and running!'

Elsie's eyes became glazed and her head started to droop. Mike was a bit worried to start with. He thought he'd poisoned her with one of his pies.

'The spirits are with us,' she said.

I predicted a sharp upturn in TITCO turnover.

Boycie was first in line. He wanted a tip for the Derby but got rather more than he bargained for. Elsie conjured up a spirit who was waving a piece of paper a bit lively and was dead keen to get in touch.

'Have you any idea who it could be?' she said.

He started to sweat. 'This piece of paper—it's not a log-book for a Cortina is it?'

It turned out to be his old man, come back to tell him to take care of his kids. Either we was in for another forty-two-carrot miracle or Marlene had a bit of explaining to do.

Next up looked like a lady, tall and slender, long, golden-brown hair. 'The fingers are covered in gold and ruby,' Elsie said. 'Bracelets adorn the wrists.'

'You know who that is, don't you?' I said.

'Sounds like Jimmy Savile,' Trigger said.

'*Jimmy Savile?* That is our mother!'

'She says she is proud of her children.' Elsie contin-

No one wants to do business with a bloke who can't stand a round of Piña Coladas.

ued. 'She says you have both worked hard to succeed, but never mind. She wants you to know that she is always with you.'

That wiped the grin off Rodney's face. He and Cassandra had been at it hammer and tongs for the best part of a month.

Then Elsie said: 'She is concerned for you, Derek. She is concerned for your health . . .'

Today's executive has learnt to live with a few pieces of bad news on the way through the University of Hard Knocks. I was stabbed outside a nightclub once. Instead of going to a doctor I dressed the wound myself with TCP and a flannel. I didn't even report the person who did it to the Old Bill. Mind you, I was engaged to her at the time. But I'm man enough to admit that Mum's message really choked me.

I spent the next few days in right lumber. Mum would hardly have bothered to come all that way to tell me I'd copped a bout of yuppy flu. It had to be a computer virus or worse . . . I swallowed hard. What of TITCO's five-year plan? All them mergers and accusations I had in mind. I always thought we would eventually go legit, and register as a proper, real McCoy company. But now . . .

I had a responsibility to my shareholders. I brought out the Filofax and factored in a full service with oil-change down the hospital.

I'm a BUPA sort of person, myself; private rooms, videos, a bit of *sacré bleu* chef and a half bottle of Geoffrey Chambertin. But there you go. Rodney had forgotten to keep up the payments, so I had to settle for a once-over by Robbie Meadows, courtesy of the National Health. Still, I like to think the black silk pyjamas caused a bit of a stir on the ward. Unfortunately, they couldn't wind up the scanner until the day Elsie was due to pull in the punters for the first pukka séance. My fellow members of the board presented themselves for a power elevenses the next morning to debrief me. Rodney slipped me a bacon sandwich under the bedclothes. They looked about as cheerful as Duncan Goodhew's barber.

'Did it all go well?' I said.

Rodney wasn't sure.

Albert was. 'It was a total cock-up from where I was standing.'

'You know those posters you put in the pub windows?' Cassandra said. 'With "The Séance" and the ghostly face?'

'Promo,' I said.

'Well, a lot of people got the wrong impression . . .'

The dozy twonks had thought 'The Séance' was a heavy metal band. So when Elsie turned up instead of Iron Maiden they weren't pleased.

'Luckily,' Rodney said, 'she remained in a trance throughout the riot.'

I was choked. 'Ain't it amazing, eh? I only organized that séance out of the goodness of my heart, and they chuck it back in my face!'

As I lay back I felt an agonizing pain. Rodney grabbed me by the shoulders.

'Hold on, Del,' he said. 'Hold on! I'll get the nurse! Don't die, Del, don't bloody die!'

It was an emotional moment for me too. I'd just sat on my bacon sandwich.

R and R is a byword at the Peckham Business School. Work hard, play hard is the way we yuppies do the business. Two days in a hospital bed ain't exactly a week in St Morris, but it has its ups and downs.

I'm big enough, in a meteorological sense, to admit that there were times when I was scared. When I thought: this time next year I'll be needing Elsie Partridge as an interpreter. When I knew the only thing between me and a nice little urn was my Cliff Richards tape and Rodney's Bulgarian Walkman.

But you don't just hand in your cards in this game, not without keeping a few up your sleeve. It's people like me who storm German machine-gun nests. So when Doctor Meadows came round with the diagnosis I said: 'Well, come on, then, tell us the worst. And don't worry, I can take it. I'm not frightened. No pulling punches, all right? I want it straight from the shoulder.'

He looked me in the eye. 'Yeah, I think it's best in the long run,' he said. 'Derek, you have an Irritable Bowel.'

'I'm not surprised,' I said, 'the way you lot have been pulling me about.'

He shook his head and explained. Apparently it's a syndrome. A lot of yuppies get it. It's the late-night international telephone calls, the fast food and faster living, the tequila sunsets, the chattering of the fax machine, the Stock Market flirtations, the upturns, the downturns, the sandwich courses, the lunch breaks, the rent arrears, the junk bonds, the bric-à-brac shops, the cut-glass goblets, the accessories . . . I could go on.

'The fact is, Derek,' he said, 'there's basically nothing wrong with you.'

I played it cool.

'*Thank God!*' I yelled. 'Thank Allah, thank Buddha . . .'

It was a miracle.'

I hadn't felt that cushty since the time I went down Our Lady of the Divine Rosary for confession. As I told Father O'Keith, I'd bought some gear off Sunglasses Ron and Paddy the Greek that wasn't entirely kosher. He looked up the price list and gave me a choice of ten Our Fathers or a donation to the St Mary's Hospice fund.

I gave the fund a score to straighten things out good and proper but discovered that they was still a

hundred and eighty-five grand short of saving the old place from demolition. Mum and Grandad checked in there before they hit the snooze button, and I wanted to keep it open long enough for them to take care of Uncle Albert. I whipped out the Filofax and set about drafting a business plan:

1. Sponsored darts match at the Nag's.
2. A raffle and all.
3. Er . . .

It was going to be bigger than Band Aid! I was well on the way to cracking it when Father O'Keith gave me a shout and pointed with a trembling finger at the statue of the Virgin and Child. I legged it over there and had a butcher's. I could hardly believe my eyes. It was more amazing than seeing Boycie buy a round of drinks. As we watched, a single tear rolled down Mary's cheek. Then another.

'It's a miracle!' Father O'Keith said.

'Yeah . . .' I said. 'You don't get many of them round Peckham!'

'It's a sign, Del.' He wasn't wrong.

'It's a sign that we can make a fortune!'

'*What?*' He was way behind.

'We have got ourselves an authentic, de-luxe miracle!' I said. 'They go for a bomb these days!'

'How can you talk about money at a time like this?'

'Well, what do you want to talk about?' I asked. 'Holidays? People will pay through the nose to see something like this. I'm talking about newspapers, magazines, television! You could have the place repaired, redecorated and get Samantha Fox to re-open it!'

His eyes lit up. 'Do you really think we could?'

'Of course. I mean she don't come cheap, but it's—'

'No, I mean save the hospice?'

'It'll be a doddle! Where's your phone?'

I briefed my people and the TITCO publicity machine rolled into action. Reuters, Tass, the BBC, the *Peckham Echo*—we even put a call through to Channel 4.

They was down the church in no time and I was handing out contracts like they was going out of style. At that rate, St Mary's Hospice wasn't just going to be saved from demolition—they'd be able to stretch to a loft conversion and a nautical gym as well. I suppose I shouldn't have been surprised when I came across the odd Doubting Thomas along the way.

'You're pulling a stroke, ain't you, Del?' Rodney said. 'There are cardinals and archbishops who've been in the business all their lives and never got a sniff of a miracle! But here you are, five minutes in the game, and you're a prophet already—profit being the operative word!'

Ah, well. As Bobby Graham once said: 'That's ELIF.'

I was on course for giving a few lectures at Wembley myself until Father O'Keith noticed that the church was short of a few roof slates. I was just giving the world's press another exclusive when he called me away for an extraordinary general meeting of the fund-raising body.

'It's raining, Del,' he said. 'The water's sweeping down the walls, along the joists and on to the statue. This isn't a miracle, it's a flaming leak!'

'That's a turn-up, ain't it?' I said.

'Someone's stolen the lead!'

I shook my head in disbelief. 'You can't trust no one these days, can you?'

'No need to worry, Father,' Rodney said helpfully, 'you're in luck. We've got loads of lead in our garage ...' He turned on me, his mind whirring. It was like something out of *The Exorcist*. 'I don't believe you, Del!'

I looked at Father O'Keith and shrugged. A prophet in his own manor ...

'That's what you bought off Sunglasses Rod and Paddy the Greek, isn't it, Derek?'

'I didn't know at the time, Father, honest. I wouldn't have touched it otherwise. That's why I had to come and confess ...'

'So you knew all along?'

'We saved St Mary's, didn't we?'

'Derek,' he said. 'Look me in the eyes. Are you telling me that, just for the sake of some small, decrepit, old building, you created this whole tissue of lies and deceit? You deliberately and willingly set out to defraud all those newspapers and television companies out of thousands and thousands of pounds?'

I bowed my head. 'Yeah . . .'

He placed both hands on my barnet.

'God bless you, my son,' he said.

Del's Dossier

TROTTERS INDEPENDENT TRADING CO.

NEW YORK
PARIS
PECKHAM

Sir John Harvey Oswald, Esq
Parallax Enterprises Ltd
P O Box 18
Herefordshire

22 March 1990

Dear Sir John,

I'll level with you. I ain't seen your new game show, TROUBLESHOOTER, cos
the TV don't work whenever I'm on the mobile phone, but my editor at BBC
Books says it's going to be a nice little earner. Enough said. I can see you
and I speak the same language, so I thought I'd drop you a quick line.

The fact is, John, though I've just delivered the ms of my new book, THE
TROTTER WAY TO MILLIONS, (you'll be chuffed to hear you feature quite
largely in it, along with Boycie, Trig, Bobby Murdoch and your old mucker
Sir Ralph Heartburn), I'm in dead stuke.

Don't put the word out, but the TITCO Express has temporarily parted
company with the fiscal rails. I've got a consignment of hooky word
processors that I'm having a bit of trouble shifting. Turkish raincoats seem
to have gone out of fashion, and I've got a cupboard fill of the bleeders.
The only bright spot on the horizon is a shipment of Brut aerosol
deodorants I've got coming in from Albania. We've all got to do our bit to
keep the workplace environmentally friendly now the hot weather's here.

The long and the short of it is: are you the man to help a small business
do its best to even up the balance of trade and put this septic isle back into the
First Division?

Even if you just took a couple of the word processors off my hands, it would
help. To you, John, I'm talking fifty quid for the both, and I'll throw in a
raincoat as a sweetener. I'll get my brother to drive them over to your
manor next week if I don't hear from you.

This ain't goodbye, so I'll just say Bonjour.

Yrs,

Del Trotter

Derek Trotter

DEREK TROTTER
Chairman and Managing Director

127 Nelson Mandela House
Nyere Estate
Peckham, London SE15

SIR JOHN HARVEY-JONES MBE
CHAIRMAN

PARALLAX ENTERPRISES LTD.
P.O. BOX 18

HEREFORDSHIRE HR9 7TL
VAT No. 467 8375 92

Derek Trotter,
T.I.T.Co, 127 Mandela House,
Peckham,
London SE15.

27th March 1990

Dear Derek

Thank you so much for your letter of the 22nd March.   I am indeed sorry
to hear that your Trotter Independent Trading is in such a tangle.

Britannia depends greatly on the support of her Trusted Independent
Traders, and would undoubtedly be very flat without them.

It seems to me that you have made a simple error in your approach to
business. In general it tends to be more effective if you buy cheaply and
sell expensively, than if you do it the other way round. Also I feel
that it is possible that your quality controls may not be performing to
their full efficiency, and that your purchasing director may be over
enthusiastic, and too anxious to clinch the deal.

I am sorry about the Turkish raincoats, but wonder whether you have
contacted Sir Ralph Heartburn? He likes a bit of Turkish stuff, and runs
through raincoats at, I understand, a record rate.

On balance, with the summer coming up, I think I'd rather try the Brut
aerosol deodorants than the word processors. However their port of origin
does cause concern. Maybe the well known Yugoslavian saying "to stink
like an Albanian goat" gives a clue to the development of the deodorant
industry in that great country. Personally I think I would look to
extended testing before buying in quantity.

With every good wish for your continued success. I also enclose a stamped
envelope for a copy of "The Trotter Way to Millions". Please mail it
express, I need the help.

Yours sincerely.

John Harvey-Com

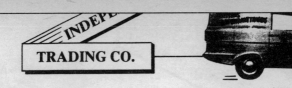

TRADING CO.

Sir John Harvey Oswald, Esq
Parallax Enterprises Ltd
P O Box 18
Herefordshire

30 April 1990

Dear Sir John,

Many thanks for yours of the 27 March. Sorry not to get back to you
sooner, but I've been offshore. Like Anita Roddick, I'm planning to take my
holidays in the Amazon as from this time next year, but for now I had to
settle for the Costa del Sol.

I'll be honest, John, it looks like your advice'll get TITCO right back on the
rollercoaster. I'll out the word out to Sir Ralph first thing next week and I
reckon between him and Anita we should be able to shift the lot. She's
doing a nice bit of business with the Amazons, and whilst I prefer readies to
Murumuru body butter, the one thing we're agreed on is: without a decent
raincoat in a Rainforest you'd be in right lumber. And worry not, my son -
from now on I'm really lumping up the margins!

The one cloud on the TITCO horizon is the consignment of Brut aerosol
deodorant. I'm just not sure it'll stand up to the sort of testing you had in
mind. I know just what you mean re: the Albanian goat. I took delivery of
two dozen leather jackets from the same source before Christmas, and not
even Brut could cure them. I eventually had to put the lot out to grass.

I can do you one favour though. I enclose a copy of the ms of THE TROTTER
WAY TO MILLIONS for your business and personal use. As with all my
merchandise, it comes with the Trotter 'Can't Lose' Guarantee.

Nigel Dawson's been pestering me to write the foreword ever since he
started on his two-day week, but I'm just not sure he's got the weight. Now
that your TV show's over, maybe you'd like to knock one out? There's a
score in it for you, or a mutton vindaloo down the Star of Bengal if you're in
the mood.

Bonne bouche for now,

Yrs, *Del Trotter*

Derek Trotter

DEREK TROTTER
Chairman and Managing Director

TROTTERS
INDEPENDENT
TRADING CO.

Charles Satchel, Esq
Satchel & Satchel Group Ltd
Lansdown House
Berkeley Square
London W1

30 March 1990

Dear Chas,

Right now I know life's treating you about the same as Paxo treats a turkey.
The FT tells me that you and Greta ain't even able to lump up on the
expenses like you used to. It's enough to make your teeth itch.

But cheer up, Charlie! I've had partnership problems myself over the
years, but in my book (it's called THE TROTTER WAY TO MILLIONS, and the
BBC are outing it this Christmas) he who dares wins. Take it from me, what
you need to stop them shares flopping like jelly on a wet mattress is a big
slice of new business - and that's where TITCO can help you out.

I've ponced around the ad game myself, as it happens. Asking me if I know
about the marketplace is like asking Mr Kipling if he knows about cakes!
So I know you'd be on an earner if you pitched for The Trotter Collection.

As an arty sort of bloke yourself, you'll appreciate the quality gear we've
selected at the House of Trotter. Parisienne haut couture fashion, superior
objets d'art and modern works of art, Chippendale tea pots, Yves Saint Dior
parfums, Georgian digital clocks, La Dolce Vita Italian men's shirts made in
Malaya - if it's got style, it's in The Trotter Collection.

The way I see it, Chas, you get out your sketch pad and knock out a few
catalogues, and I'll let you have the merchandise at cost. We can split the
profits straight down the middle, sixty/forty.

Just give me the nod and I'll send my brother Rodney over with the van.

A bain marie,

Yrs, *Del Trotter*

No Reply!

Derek Trotter

DEREK TROTTER
Chairman and Managing Director

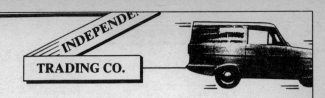

INDEPENDEN[T]

TRADING CO.

Barry Hearn, Esq
Matchroom
10 Western Road
Romford
Essex
RM1 3JT

6 May 1990

Dear Barry,

What a choker! I saw your boy Steve go down in the World Championship as I was putting the finishing touches to my book THE TROTTER WAY TO MILLIONS (The BBC are outing it at Christmas) and thought: this is the end of an era. It was the end of a tenner and all - not that I'm a gambling man.

I know you'll be right with me when I say there's no such thing as luck (I mean, if there was, you'd hardly have your HQ in Romford, would you?), but we was robbed!

Since we're both a bit out of pocket as a result, I thought I'd give you the chance to invest in a scheme that'll put us back amongst the big breaks. My brother Rodney says you got into the perfume business a few years back, so the new international fragrance from The House of Trotter will be just your oeuf en cocotte. It's a bit like Brut, but we at TITCO call it 'Boardroom', on account of it smells pretty powerful.

I've got a containerload coming in from Albania any minute, and I've a hunch it'll go down a storm with the boys now the hot weather's here.

How much shall I put you down for?

This ain't goodbye, so I'll just say eau de toilette.

Yrs, *Del Trotter*

Derek Trotter

DEREK TROTTER
Chairman and Managing Director
127 Nelson Mandela House
Nyere Estate
Peckham, London SE15

MATCHROOM

Our ref: BH/MM   14 May 1990.

Derek Trotter,
127 Nelson Mandela House
Peckham,
SE15.

Dear Del,

Nice to hear from you - I wasn't sure anyone in South London could
write!

Love the idea of the new fragrance, put me down for the first case tha[t]
falls off the back of your lorry!

Yours sincerely,

Barry Hearn.

MATCHROOM LIMITED
VAT REG. No. 1731858
Directors: BARRY HEARN, STEVE DAVIS, JIMMY WHITE, NEAL FOULDS,
CLIFF THORBURN, TERRY GRIFFITHS, DENNIS TAYLOR,
WILLIE THORNE, TONY MEO, STEVE DAWSON

10 WESTERN ROA[D]
ROMFORD, ESSE[X]

Mr. Trump is in receipt of your business presentation.

While he appreciates your bringing this opportunity to his
attention, regretfully, it is of no interest to him at the present
time. We will be happy to keep your proposal on file so that if the
opportunity presents itself, we will certainly be in touch.

Thank you for writing Mr. Trump, and we wish you much
success in your endeavors.

THE TRUMP ORGANIZATION

 **TRADING CO.**

Richard Branston, Esq
Virgin Group Ltd
120 Campden Hill Road
London W8 7AR

25 March 1990

Dear Ricky,

I hear the Good Ship Branston's hit a bit of fiscal turbulence. Eau de vie!
I've had days like that! Which of us hasn't, in the media game? So cheer
up! If TITCO ever hits a bare market I hang up the mobile phone, slip into
the roll-neck and sheepskin with forty-two carrot accessories, and head
down the Nag's.

Take a leaf out of my book, Ricardo (it's called THE TROTTER WAY TO
MILLIONS, and BBC Books will be outing it at Christmas), at times like this,
it's all about *image*. Crack a Tia-Maria-and-Lucozade and a couple of
Castellas on the slate, give the barmaid a small that'll knock her bandy, and
you'll be off the rocks in no time.

The way I see it, them pullovers are where your troubles start. I mean,
bless me gently, what's an aspiring tycoon doing in a Val Doonican jumper?
I know Frank Bough's got a bit of a reputation for doing the business, but
that don't mean you have to dress like him!

This is where The Trotter Collection comes to the rescue. We have access to
an exclusive range of Bulgarian navy blue three piece suits, for starters.
Match them up with a navy shirt, white tie and loafers, a chunky bracelet
and a medallion and bingo, you're what we call highly geared! If a trendy
green trenchcoat and an Arnie Becker aluminium briefcase are more your
menage a trois, look no further! If you haven't had to flog the island,
perhaps something casual - a Vinyl shirt, a Barber and a hint of zebra-skin.

The Trotter Collection. Whatever the occasion, we'll really fit you up! Like
yourself, I'm a readies man, but we can settle it on the weekly until you're
back on the big dipper.

In the meantime, son et lumiere, as we say in the fashion world.

Yrs, *Del Trotter*

Derek Trotter

Send your order to: **DEREK TROTTER**
                          Chairman and Managing Director
                          127 Nelson Mandela House

Virgin

120 Campden Hill Road, London W8 7AR
Tel: 01-229 1282 Telex: 8954617
Fax: 01-727 8200

3 April 1990

As From 6th May
Tel: 071-229 1282
Fax: 071-727 8200

Derek Trotter
Trotters Independent Trading Co
127 Nelson Mandela House
Peckham SE15

Dear Derek

Thanks very much but, no thanks.

Kind regards

pp *Sarah Hopley*

Richard Branson
Chairman
Virgin Group of Companies

Sarah Hopley, Esq
Virgin Group Ltd
120 Campden Hill Road
London W8 7AR

6 April 1990

Dear Sarah,

Thanks for yours of the 3 April.

So, Ricardo Branston got the old heave-ho, eh? Well, I hate to say I told him so. It was the pullovers, see. And to think that a small investment in The Trotter Collection could have put him right back in the First Division. I mean, Sir John Harvey-Oswald sports a Bulgarian three-piece with a range of neckwear you can't ignore and there's no stopping him.

Now you're Chairman, Sarah, don't make the same mistake. As one chief exec to another, I'm sure you won't mind me giving you a few tips on stronging it in the boardroom.

1. Be careful who you're seen coming back from Magaluf with. It's OK to let your hair down offshore, but don't let the paparazzi snap you with a bloke who don't know the Don Jones Index from a hole in the head.

2. Try not to have

TROTTERS
INDEPENDENT
TRADING CO.

Bobby Murdoch Esq
SKY TV, PLC
6 Centaurs Business Park
Isleworth
TW

14 May 1990

Dear Bobby,

I ain't ever seen Sky TV cos I left our new satellite dish on the kitchen table
and Uncle Albert stir-fried a prawn curry in it, but I've heard you're in
stuke. Take a tip from me, my son, as one specialist to another. The
Monopoly Commission are busy people. You don't want to bother them.

I get itchy fever just thinking about what might happen if they took a
butcher's at TITCO. We've cornered the market in Albanian Brut aerosol
deodorant, Turkish raincoats and hand-bottled Yves Saint Dior parfums. I'm
the Bonker Hunt of the eau de toilette world.

I've run the figures through the software, Bobby, and the good news is I
think I might just be able to help you out. I've ponced about in the media
game myself, now and again, and always meant to take over a radio station
or two. I'm sure you feel the same about Parisienne haut couture, Georgian
digital clocks and hooky washing powder. I'm not going to ask you for cash
on the hip - why don't we just do a swap?

Just say the word, and I'll send my brother Rodney round with the
merchandise. He can pick up your satellite dishes at the same time. The
Monopoly boys won't know what hit them!

This ain't goodbye, so I'll just say g'day.

Yrs, *Del Trotter*   *No Reply!*

Derek Trotter

PS. Does the name Jumbo Mills mean anything to you?

DEREK TROTTER
Chairman and Managing Director
127 Nelson Mandela House

All trade enquiries to:

DEREK TROTTER
127 Nelson Mandela House
Nyere Estate
Peckham, London SE15

LIKE MOST JAPANESE, TITCO started small.

TITCO COUNTRY – The Peckham Business School campus.

POWER BREAKFASTING AT Nelson Mandela House – *another* letter from Sir John Harvey-Oswald...

THE TROTTER GUARANTEE: All my merchandise is straight. This lot's straight from a house in the country.

IN THE SIXTIES there were
Mods . . .

. . . THERE WERE Rockers
. . .

. . . AND THERE WAS
Rodney.

OUR FINANCIAL DIRECTOR – coming to grips with the new technology.

IN THE BOARDROOM, body language is extremely important.

RODNEY LEARNT THE art of seduction by watching *Wildlife on One*.

BOYCIE'S DONE TIME for perjury, embezzlement, conspiring to pervert the course of justice, the fraudulent conversion of traveller's cheques and attempting to bribe the Mayor of Lambeth. With that lot on his CV, no wonder all the merchant banks are after him.

SOME PEOPLE ARE born a halfpenny short of a shilling. In Trig's case, God added VAT.

THERE'S NO BUSINESS like show business!

VERY WALL STREET: very Trotter.

TITCO – POISED TO seize the initiative in the global marketplace

AFTERWARDS . . .

CHAPTER FIVE

A Bird in the Hand

You only have to glance at the social columns of the *FT* to see the great achievers as they go about the bizzo. Hanging off the arm of every great tycoon is the bird he's hiked up with—and I bet you a pound to a penny it's a sort so hot it'd take Red Adair to put her out. These birds ain't your two halves of Stingo, a packet of pork scratchings and Bob's your uncle rubbish neither. These birds are *class*—girls with a big pair of lungs on them, the kind you'd be proud to be seen in a Berni with.

The fact is, power attracts. Big wallets blag the big bazumbas. That's why you've got your oil magnates like Alan Khoshaggi and Sheik Yermoney stronging it with right brammas. That's why when Sir Ralph Heartburn brings his girl back from Tenerife it doesn't take him two weeks to get her out of quarantine.

I mean, let's face it, no way is someone like Peter De Samurai going to get himself lumbered on his yacht with some old bow-wow who doesn't know the difference between a Liebfraumilk and a can of Tizer.

You never saw old Harry Onassis so embarrassed by the look of his bird he had to tell the boys he was taking her to market. So it will come as no surprise to you to hear that I'm being a bit choosy these days.

I'm going to come clean. It wasn't always like that. I've probably had more dogs in my time than Crufts.

I had a hot date once with a sort I'd been told looked like the one in Abba. How was I to know they meant the bloke with the moustache? She was so fat she'd have needed to go on a diet to get in the Roly Polies. Still, it all went down on the CV.

You learn from your mistakes. Mainly, beware of Australians. Apart from that, all you have to know about women is, treat them with respect. Always take them out for a meal they won't forget. Mutton vindaloo never fails.

'Course, the approach of the successful tycoon is always going to mark him out from first-rung management. In the old days, Rodney was blown out more times than a wind sock. Before he married Cassandra he was covered in bruises—where the girls kept pushing him away with ten-foot barge-poles.

There was a few exceptions. Monica with the fat thighs for starters; she looked as though she was bopping the night away in jodhpurs. Then there was

It ain't all beer and skittles, making billion-pound decisions.

Miss Anabolic Steroids, aka Big Brenda, the Southern Areas shot putt champion. I think he went off her just 'cos she was taller than him.

Part of his trouble was he had what leading psychiatrists call 'a thing about uniforms'. The other part is, he's a total pranny. Some of his dates arrived by skateboard. Take that little thing he took to the pictures when he was twenty—he was lucky not to get his collar felt. He says she swore blind to him she was sixteen. How was he to know she was only nine?

'She was sixteen that month!' he protested. 'I didn't suspect anything till she paid her fare with a school bus pass. Anyway, she did all the chatting up. She asked me to take her.'

'She had to, didn't she?' I said. 'They wouldn't let her in without an adult.'

I like my women with more, well . . . lungs that'd bruise your ribs. I dropped Rodney at the evening institute the other night and was just about to drive off when I saw a couple of real sorts get out of a Porsche and scamper into a wine bar. Right brammas they were. No doubt about it, I thought, that's a bit for me!

I pulled my stomach in and tightened the belt of my trendy green trenchcoat. These birds are health conscious. They're fully conversant with the Peckham Business School staple: tough in the boardroom, tough in the bedroom.

The place was full of yuppy sorts. You can't go wrong in a place like that. Nowadays these young Eurobirds go for mature men, men who have made it in life. All you've got to do is learn to speak their language. They don't talk proper English like what we do. I've been earholing them. It's all 'ya' and 'sooper' and 'fab'. And you've got to talk about money all the time. It's their favourite subject. You chat about readies and it really impresses them.

Here's a good opener: 'It's all go when you're in a high-profile business, ain't it? I'm in stocks and shares myself. I bought a few thousand percentage points in a little department store this afternoon. Now I've got to let my lawyer and accountant know. Gives you the hump, don't it? How do you spell Harrods anyway?' Take it from me, that's you up and running.

No doubt about it, this was definitely my kind of place. Marble-topped tables with wrought-iron legs, that sort of thing. I strolled over towards the two sorts at the bar. It was only a matter of time before they recognized that I was one of them. I held my Filofax prominently as I made my way towards them, smiling and nodding to a few fellow yuppies as I passed.

'Oh, it's good to unwind, ain't it?' I said wearily.

'Sorry?' the blonde one said.

'After a day in the City—it's good to unwind.'

'I imagine it must be very tiring.'

'Tiring? I'm cream crackered and that's no lie! I've

been up since six this morning trying to talk to a bloke in New York.'

'Why didn't you use a telephone?'

I brought out my Nomad. 'No, no, I've got a phone and all that! I meant, it's a long and stressful day in the old commodities market. It's a git of a journey back to the penthouse as well. I buy and sell whatever's going. Iron ore. Sugarbeet. I made a killing today in olive oil. God knows what Popeye'll say when he gets home!'

I had a good laugh at that one, but they were a bit slow on the uptake.

The barman came over and asked me if I wanted a drink.

I moved in for the kill. My knowledge of the noble grape would knock 'em bandy.

'Yes,' I said. 'I think I'll have a bottle of Beaujolais Nouveau.'

'Yes, sir.'

I paused a moment, then called him back.

'Make it a '79,' I said.

The girls burst out laughing. Funny how long it takes some people to get the joke, ain't it?

'Oh, Popeye? You got it, did you?' I let them have it with my Bobby Ewing smile. I was well in there. 'That was a good one, wasn't it?'

Unless you've got my *servir frais mais non glacé* with the ladies, you will simply never make it into the upper stratos of the business world. Let's cast a side-long glance at Rodney again.

'I frighten them off,' he announced one night.

'Frighten them off?' Uncle Albert asked.

'He's got a thing about uniforms,' I explained.

'It's got nothing to do with uniforms,' he said. 'I got over that phase months ago. Look, it may be that to morons like Mickey Pearce a woman is not another person, someone to talk to, someone to relate to. A woman is just a lump of decoration to bolster their macho image, a trinket to hang on the arm to prove their masculinity. Well, I'm different!'

Albert and I looked at each other. What would Mum have thought?

'No, no, no! I mean, I either like a girl, or I don't. If I don't like her, I don't see her no more. But if I do like her, I tend to get ... well, you know, serious. And that's what frightens them off. They're young, they want to see a bit of life—and they don't need a wally like me drooling round them. I just fall in love too easy, that's my trouble.'

According to Albert that's always been a family trait. Us Trotters wear our hearts on our sleeves. Except for Rodney, who until then had always kept his in his Wranglers.

'You don't even know what love is, Rodney,' I had to tell him. 'You ain't had enough experience to know.'

'I bet you have though, ain't you, Del?'

Some things you can't hide. 'Me? I know all about it, bruv! Covered in emotional scars, I am.'

'I was in love once,' Uncle Albert said to no one in particular.

'You see, Rodney,' I confided, 'I have this—this vision of love. I see me and my sweetheart running towards each other, in slow motion, across a field of buttercups. We're both dressed all in white, and I've done a bit of weight. Somewhere Semprini's orchestra plays the theme music from *Doctor Zhivago* . . . I was even a New Man once.'

Albert stood up with a faraway look in his eyes and walked off towards his bedroom. I thought it might be shellshock.

'Where's he going?' I said.

'I think he's just gone to be sick.'

'Oi, listen and learn, will you? Other times I see us sitting atop an Alpine peak. Looking out over the mountains and forests, it's as if we're the only two people left in the world. In the background a lone violin is playing.'

'Semprini on a skiing holiday, I suppose?' Rodney's lip curled. 'That's not a vision of love, it's more like a yoghurt commercial!'

I sighed. 'You've got a lot to learn, Rodney. I try and give you the benefit of my experience and you throw it in my face!'

Albert returned from his bedroom carrying a photograph of one of his old battleships.

'Which one's this?'

'Helga!'

'Helga? Helga who?'

'I loved her,' he said, his eyes misting over. 'I don't think I ever really stopped loving her.'

Rodney checked his watch. 'Yeah, well, it's getting a bit . . .'

'It was 1946,' Albert went on. 'We'd sailed to Hamburg to pick up prisoners of war. Helga was working in a bar near the docks. She was the most beautiful woman I'd ever seen—I fell in love with her the moment I saw her!' He gave a sentimental smile. 'The little finger on her right hand was missing!'

'Ah, bless her,' Rodney said.

'Get it caught in the till, did she?' I said.

'No,' he said. 'She lost it when her home was bombed. Her entire family was wiped out.'

That wiped the smile from my face.

'I asked her to marry me. She said no. Just like that, no. See, I'd mistook her gestures of friendship as tokens of love. I suppose it was all for the best really. The authorities didn't like the idea of us fraternizing with the Germans, and I was still married to your Aunt Ada and she'd have kicked up a stink. It's funny, you know, but even after all these years, if I'm

watching a war film and I hear the word "*nein*", I always think of Helga.'

'"Cos that's how many fingers she had?' Rodney asked.

'It's the German for "no". I'll put this photo back in my box.'

'Yeah, keep it safe, eh!' I said.

Uncle Albert stopped in the doorway, turned, and looked at us with his sad old eyes.

'I think in her own way she loved me,' he said. 'She never used to charge me as much as the other lads!'

Ah, romance. Sir Ralph Heartburn probably won't agree with me here, but I often wonder whether you can really mix it with business.

I won't ever forget the time I took up with Pauline again. She'd been my fiancée years back, when we were Mods. It was love's young dream. The only reason she left me was because she met a bloke with a faster Vespa.

By the time I met her second time around the poor girl had had two husbands die on her. 'One more and she gets to keep the match ball,' Rodney said a bit unsympathetically.

The night we got engaged he didn't exactly bust a blood vessel congratulating me. 'Triffic,' he said, 'we'll have to make an announcement in the *Exchange and Mart*.'

'But you haven't heard the best part,' I said. 'This is a double celebration. Not only have I got hitched but my bride-to-be has kindly condescended to come and live with us!'

Things went downhill from there. I didn't mind so much that Pauline'd cook me fillet steak whilst Rodney and Albert had to share a tin of corned beef—I mean, rank has its privileges—but when she wanted to tear me away from the TITCO HQ, my powerbase, I had to remind her that I had a position to maintain in the business community.

'Buy a house?' I said. 'I can't! Don't you see, the moment I put my signature on any document the authorities are going to know that I'm alive!'

She was unmoved. 'You can do what my other husbands did, put the house in my name. Nobody's going to think it strange me buying a house, not with all the money I got on the life insurance.' She paused. 'Have you got your life insured, Del?'

Never pull birds too early in the game—you'll have to buy them drinks all night.

As a matter of fact I hadn't. I'd never felt like dying before.

'We'll have to sort that out,' she said. 'A wife needs protection.'

'Specially with your luck, Pauline,' Rodney said.

My bride-to-be wasn't in the mood for any banter. She headed for the door.

'I'm just popping down to the jewellers to put a deposit on that ring I saw,' she said to me.

'Another one?' Rodney gasped. 'You've been engaged five times and married twice. You must have more rings than Bravington's! What is it with you? Are you trying to corner the world's gold market, or have you just got a thing about wedding cakes?'

Whilst Pauline was busy making a take-over bid for Ratner's, I got to thinking. The insurance question worried me. And when Trig called to say that her last husband had died of food poisoning, I knew I had to do a runner with the other key members of the TITCO board.

Business or pleasure, I've always found that when you're making a tactical withdrawal it's best to leave the door open behind you. I knew I had to break my decision to Pauline gently.

I left a note: 'You've got five clear days to get out of the flat, and don't ever come back, you money-grabbing old murderess,' it read. 'All my love, Del Boy. And a few kisses.'

Then I had it away on my toes before she had a chance to come back with the deadly nightshade.

We stayed away for five days and returned to

Nelson Mandela House expecting her to burst out of one of the rooms any moment, brandishing her mother-of-pearl-handled flick knives. It could have been *Psycho* in a tower block.

But Pauline was nowhere to be seen. All the beds were neatly made, she'd even been round with the hoover! It didn't half look clean and tidy in the kitchen. What was her game then? I thought, there's no way Pauline would just leave without doing something nasty to me.

'I've got a confession to make,' Rodney said. 'You know that phone call from Trigger? The one about food poisoning and police investigations? Well, it was a wind-up. Me and Grandad put him up to it . . . We did it for you, Del Boy.'

'You couple of . . . of . . . rascals!' I said.

'Got you out of stuke, didn't it?'

It certainly had, but show me the businessman who hasn't had the odd leg-up along the way.

That's when I found her letter. The contents were a bit iffy for me to bother you with, but I'll tell you how she signed it off: 'PS,' it said, 'don't forget to put the receiver back on the hook.'

The cow. What had I ever done to *her*? She'd phoned the talking clock before she left.

'We've been connected for . . . Gordon Bennett, the letter was dated four days ago!' Call it a fifth sense,

call it what you like, but I had a very funny feeling about this.

'I don't want to worry you, Del,' Rodney said, 'but this speaking clock's got an American accent!'

CHAPTER SIX

That's Entertainment

At the Peckham Business School we've got a saying: when Bobby Murdoch goes down a road, watch closely. If he don't come back, follow. I reckon that's where Colonel 'Ernie' Sanders came unstuck; he should have been shelling out for TV stations, not distilleries.

I know the day I finally outed all them storm-damaged umbrellas I was seriously tempted to invest in some Argentinian satellite dishes, perhaps even have a punt at the *Peckham Echo*, but now I'm glad I waited. The regional franchises are up for grabs again soon, and I reckon I'll be well in with Radio TITCO.

I've been a bit of an impresario since way back. I

In the movie business, it's all about essential ingredients— suspense, lots of killings and a bit of humpty dumpty —and treating your creative people to a bit of haute couture to keep morale up.

even tried to make Rodney into a child star. I enrolled him in tap-dancing school, but his legs let him down. So did his Doc Martens. He made 'Zippidy Doo Dah' sound like the advance on Leningrad.

Someone—probably Sir John Harvey-Oswald—once said there's no such thing as a free lunch. Well, I'm here to tell you he wasn't talking about the entertainment business. I mean, you only had to take a butcher's at Rupert Maxwell to see that he was not short of a plate of egg and chips. I've got a hunch that if you're right at the top of the media heap, you can really lump up on the expenses.

I've always been a petty cash man myself, so I've felt right at home in the showbiz circus. In fact, I spotted a bit of a media opportunity down the Nag's only last year. Everyone was there: Trig, Boycie, Rodney, Mickey Pearce, his new bird—the whole Peckham rat pack.

'What's the matter with you, Boycie?' Trig was saying as he put down his cards. 'You don't seem your old self tonight. You ain't cheated once.'

'You've no idea what it's like to have a wife who can't have children,' Boycie said. 'I've tried consoling her. I said, "Marlene, God didn't mean you to have kids, so shut up about it." But it didn't help. Next week we're down for another going over at that bloody hospital. Embarrassing ain't the word. I'm sure they do half them tests for a giggle. I mean,

she's the one with the problem, so why have I got to go?'

I didn't want to go into details in front of Rodney. If he knew Boycie was in for a read of *Mayfair* and a quick Jodrell on the National Health, I'd never get him back down the market. He'd be off at the doctor's claiming to be infantile.

Mickey Pearce joined us with Amanda. The state of that girl! You could pick up BBC2 on her hair, and God knows what you might pick up on the rest of her. I think Mickey read my mind. Anyway, I saw his lips move.

'You know how it is,' he grinned, a bit sheepish. 'Every so often a person fancies a bit of rough.'

'And she picked you!' I said.

'Very funny. What you having, Rodney?'

'Half of lager, please.'

'Make that a big pint!' Mickey insisted, pulling out a wad.

'What you been up to?' Rodney asked.

'I'm working for Boycie, ain't I?' Mickey said. 'Delivering, picking up. He's in the video game in a big way. Pirates, naughties, all that. It's cash in hand, no questions, sweet as a nut. Where you bin, out on the knocker?'

'No, I've just come back from my evening class,' Rodney said. 'Remember I told you we'd applied for an Arts Council grant? Well, we got it! Ten thousand pounds to make a local community film. We've got all the equipment, everything—and guess who's in charge of the project?'

'You're putting me on!'

'No, it's yours truly! Mr Stevens has asked me to come up with the idea and delegate the various responsibilities to the other students.'

'Well, put me in, won't you? I'm a member of your art group.'

'Give over, Mickey, you only came one night—and that was just 'cos I told you we had a nude model.'

'Yeah, and I thought it'd be a bird. You've got to write it, Rodney. You're a natural when it comes to the written word. I'll never forget that thing you wrote some years back. What was it called?'

' "The Indictment".'

'Would have made a triffic book. Why didn't you send it to a publisher?'

'I'll be completely honest with you, Mickey. I couldn't think of a single publisher who'd understand what I was saying.'

As Mickey moved off down the bar, I was beginning to sniff what we in the business call a bit of an opening. Either that, or our visit to the zoo earlier that day had left its mark on Uncle Albert. He'd just got back from humping bales of hay around, and didn't he go on about it.

'While you've been poncing around at your soppy

art class,' he moaned to Rodney, 'I've had to unload two ton of hay!'

'Poncing around, is that what you call it?' Rodney said. 'Well, for your information I have been commissioned to make a film.'

'Give over.' Boycie laughed. 'I wouldn't leave you to make a jelly! I've heard rumours that Mickey Mouse wears a Rodney Trotter wristwatch!'

'It's true, I'm telling you. I've got all the equipment. I'm writing it and Mickey Pearce is directing.'

'Mickey Pearce?' I said. 'That dildo couldn't direct a seagull to the coast.'

'He's got experience in films,' Rodney protested.

'What, that Saturday morning job on the photographic counter at Boots? Anyway, how are you ever going to write a film? "The Indictment" never got published, did it?'

'No, 'cos you chucked it down the bloody chute!'

True, but that was only because I didn't want to see him disappointed. It was a stupid story—no murders, nothing.

'It was an indictment of a failing system!' Rodney went on. 'All right, it was a first effort—it may not have had the same social impact as, say, *Cathy Come Home* . . .'

'You're not wrong there,' I said. 'It didn't have the same social impact as *Lassie Come Home*!'

'So who's going to be in the film?' Uncle Albert asked.

Rodney nodded down the bar at the group of sorts clustered round Mickey Pearce. 'Well, all them birds for a start!'

'That was a shrewd move on your part, Rodney,' I said. 'You're the writer and Micky's the director. So he gets the casting couch and you get the biro!'

Rodney was sitting at the kitchen table awaiting inspiration when I came home next day. I was carrying a large package covered in brown paper.

'Oi, Oscar, I've got a present for you!' I said.

'What is it?'

'Close your eyes.'

'Come on, Del. I bet Tom Stoppard don't have to put up with all this!'

I pulled away the wrapping to reveal a beautiful vintage Remington. Lovely machine it was; they probably typed the Magna Carta on it.

Rodney opened his eyes and stared blankly.

'Well?' I said.

'Yeah . . . em . . . it's, er . . . it's a typewriter.'

'See that, Albert?' I said. 'He recognized it immediately. That's the author in him! You'll soon have that old screenplay knocked out now, Rodders.'

'It's a bit old, isn't it?'

'They made stuff to last in them days. That is

quality, Rodney. Look at that crest—by Royal Appointment.'

'Oh, yeah . . . "Victoria Regina".'

'Away you go then, start typing. Be creative!'

'I can't just be creative at the drop of a hat,' he moaned. 'There are certain things a writer needs before he can actually begin writing. Like a story.'

'I've got a good idea for a story. It's a bloody good one an' all. It's a sort of *Jaws*-type film.'

'*Jaws*? It's been done.'

'But this is different. It's called *There's a Rhino Loose in the City*.'

'*There's a Rhi* . . . A rhino? *There's a Rhino Loose in* . . . A *rhino*? As in rhinoceros?'

'Yeah. *There's a Rhino Loose in the City*. See, this rhinoceros escapes from a zoo and heads straight for London. Well, within days they're finding bodies lying about, but no one knows who's doing it. So they call this detective in—sort of Charlton Heston-type geezer—to solve the crimes. Now, the zoo keeper is an attractive young woman. Well, before you know where you are Charlton's giving the sort what for, and there's your romantic interest!'

'A rhinoceros?'

'Yeah, but they don't know it's missing!'

'But how can you *not* know? If you've got a rhino-ceros and one morning it ain't there—well, you know it's missing! What about the eight million people living in London? Don't none of them spot it?'

'Yes! But the ones who see it end up trampled to death!'

'What about all the others—like people in offices and cafés, people sitting on top of buses? I mean, it's a rhino!'

'He only comes out at night.'

'What is it,' Uncle Albert chipped in, 'a vampire rhino? Where does it live during the day?'

'In a lock-up garage down a back street.'

'What, he's leasing it?' Rodney asked.

'It's a disused garage where no one ever goes. The detective does find it, but it's at night.'

'And the rhino's gone out?'

'Right. So he's still no closer to solving it. You see, Rodney, this is not *just* a love story. It's also an who-dun-it.'

'An who-dun-it? What do you mean, an who-dun-it? We know who dun it. The rhino dun-it.'

'*We*, the audience, know that, but the actors don't!' I bet Steve Steelbird never had this trouble down the studio.

'This is something! A rhinoceros has escaped from a zoo. There's three hundred dead bodies covered in rhinoceros footprints. There's a lock-up garage two and a half foot deep in rhino crap and Charlton Heston suspects the butler!'

All right, I will admit there were a few snags.

'It's a disaster movie,' I explained.

'Disaster? It's a calamity, Del! Why is he killing people?'

'Well, what d'you want him to be—a social worker? He's a man-eater, ain't he?'

'No, rhinoceroses ain't carnivorous. They're vegetarians.'

'Oh, well, we'll elbow the lock-up. We'll have him hiding in the back of an health-food shop.'

'And he wouldn't head for the city, either.'

'But he's got to head for the city so he can kill lots of people.'

'His natural habitat would be open country.'

'So what are you suggesting? We call the film *There's a Rhino Loose Somewhere Out in the Sticks Where No Sod Lives*? Listen, you don't call the likes of Charlton Heston in 'cos something's eating the carrots. I just wanted to put an idea in your head, Rodney. Now I wish it'd been a bleeding bullet!'

'Anyway,' he said helpfully, 'I've only got a small budget.'

'But that's the beauty of it, Rodders. I know where there's a rhinoceros going cheap!'

'I have the kernel of an idea,' Rodney announced a few days later. That was good news. We could wait until it turned into a nut and then get on the blower to Barry Norman.

'It's what *writers* call the gestation period.'

'And what do you call it?'

Rodney chose to ignore me.

'Where's your director then?' I asked.

'He is acquainting himself with the video camera and equipment.'

'He certainly is,' I said. 'He's down the Town Hall filming a wedding.'

'What do you mean, he's filming a wedding?'

I explained. I'd been down the town hall and around a few churches taking notes of the banns. Then I'd contacted a few brides and asked if they'd like their happiest day recorded for fifty quid a throw. I'd gone into production.

'I don't believe you're doing this to me!'

'Rodney, Mickey's got to practise with that camera, ain't he? Make sure he can get it in focus and that. So why not earn while you learn, that's what I say. And he nicks all the video tapes off Boycie!'

'But, Del, this is an opportunity for me and all you're doing is making money out of it.'

'He's only got two or three weddings to do,' I said. 'Couple of christenings and he'll be finished.'

'You're just abusing the trust shown in me.'

I handed him a tenner. 'There's your share.'

'I don't want it.'

'Please yourself . . .'

'Oh, all right,' he said. 'Just this once.'

A few nights later we were eating down the Golden Lotus when in came Boycie and Marlene to collect a take-away. Boycie was banging on at her about hospitals and didn't clock for a second or two that we were there.

'Look, Marlene, I keep telling you, them doctors don't know everything. They're a bunch of chancers, that's all . . . Oh, good evening, Derek. I didn't realize you and your family were dining out.'

'Hello, darling, how are you?' I patted Marlene's tummy. 'My little godson in there yet?'

In the movie business, it's all about who you know. Abdul's cousin's girlfriend's brother's mate is a gamekeeper at one of these private zoos. And Monkey Harris's sister's husband's first wife's stepfather works for an animal food company. Put the two together, with Albert to do the donkey work, and you end up with a nice bit of bunce.

'No, he ain't—and he ain't likely to be with this husband of mine around! They've just discovered there's nothing wrong with me. It's him!'

'What's the matter then, Boycie?' I asked with concern. 'You ain't a noofter, are you?'

'See what you've started now, Marlene? Even the doctors ain't allowed to discuss this outside the confines of the laboratory. And you're holding a public debate in a Chinese take-away.'

'He's got what doctors call a low count.'

'Don't want to buy a calculator, do you?' I inquired.

'Not that sort of low count, Del. I mean he's got—'

At that moment Mr Chin brought in their order.

'Prawn balls, Mr Boyce?'

Boycie glared, daring any of us to say a word.

'It's our anniversary next Friday,' Marlene said. 'Twenty years—gawd, that's something to celebrate, ain't it? Anyway, we've hired the pub and you're all invited. By the way, is that right you're making a movie, Rodney? I used to act when I was younger. Someone actually said once that I had a promising career in films.'

'Yeah, then talkies came along and ruined it!' Boycie said. 'Let's go, Marlene!'

'Well, well, well,' I said when they'd gone. 'So Boycie's a Jaffa.'

'A Jaffa?' Uncle Albert asked.

'Seedless.'

Rodney looked as though he was thinking. 'You know, I might be able to use Boycie's problem as a

104

theme for my film. That hospital they attend is one of the leading centres for genetic research. Artificial insemination and all that . . . I mean, that's interesting, ain't it?'

'Oh, edge-of-your-seat stuff!' I said. 'Have you thought no more about the rhino?'

'I'm not bloody doing a film about a blood-sucking rhinoceros and a divvy detective! No, that hospital interests me.'

'I don't reckon they should be allowed to do it,' Albert weighed in. 'Freezing things and all that. They're messing around with nature.'

'They are not messing around with nature,' Rodney said. 'They are assisting nature. See, they only freeze the ova, or eggs, until they are ready to be fertilized. Then they take the egg and sort of mix it up with this and that and . . .'

'Yeah?' I snapped. 'Then I suppose they make an omelette. I tell you, a few years from now a young married couple thinking about starting a family won't bother going to the doctor's, they'll take a stroll down Bejams.'

A week later, Rodney was still seated in front of the vintage Remington. He had a large pile of fresh typing paper at his side, and a tiny pile of finished pages. John had days like that when we was writing *The Trotter Way to Millions*. I took it we were still at the gestation stage.

'Getting on all right, Rodney?'

'The T and the A are missing.'

'Well, that's no problem is it?'

'Well, it is if you want to write words like "at".'

'You'll find a way round it, Rodney—I've got faith in you. I tell you what, your movie ain't half caused a stir round here. You wouldn't believe how many actors and actresses live locally. I don't mean professionals, but great untapped talent! Well, I made a list of them . . .'

I handed him several sheets of paper.

'Del, you're not suggesting I use all these people in my film?'

'Just extras, that's all. Don't think about the quantity, think about the quality!'

'I'm thinking about the money, Del.'

'I said a tenner a day.'

'I can't afford to pay them a tenner a day!'

I smiled. 'They pay *us* a tenner a day!'

'You're just exploiting people.'

'I've given them your word now, Rodney. Just extras, that's all . . . And here's a list of local businesses you might like to mention.'

'The Seventh Heaven Sauna Parlour?'

'Just a mention. "Relaxing atmosphere, nice and friendly service"—that sort of thing. Did I put the undertakers down?'

'No.'

'Well, bear it in mind.'

'Del Boy, why are you putting me through this? I had high hopes when I started this project! Mr Stevens said if it was good enough it might be shown at the National Film Theatre.'

'What you worrying about? You're earning, ain't you? Listen, must shoot, got to meet a client, might be another booking. Tell me, what *is* a "natural birth"?'

I went out as Mickey and his bird came in with the video gear. I don't know why, but I could swear Amanda was wearing a nurse's uniform underneath her coat.

We was on our way down the Nag's for a preview of a new movie Boycie was distributing when Rodney had another anxiety attack.

'What's happening?' he moaned. 'What the bloody hell's happening? I've only just got the first draft off to Mr Stevens, but already I'm lumbered with more extras than Cecil B. de Mille. I've got a cast of thousands, enough advertising to see off Pearl & Dean, and now all Mickey wants to make is *Emmanuelle in Peckham*. It's getting out of hand.'

'That's showbiz, Rodders,' I said cheerfully, but I was a bit worried about Mickey Pearce. I could take or leave Mickey on the whole, but as long as he was employed by Trotter Broadcasting I didn't want anything going wrong with him. It's a hard school, the movie business, and the Driscoll Brothers had the dodgy end of the video market sewn up, with Boycie looking after the box office. If Mickey tried to muscle in on their turf, they'd hit him with a breach of copyright action that'd make *Nightmare on Elm Street* look like a stroll down memory lane.

As soon as Rodney sloped through the door, the pub went quiet.

Mike was the first to speak. 'Of all the bars in all the world and you had to walk into mine!' I had a hunch he was going to need an understudy. He sounded as though he was doing an impression of an electric blender.

'Are you in my film as well, Mike?' Rodney said wearily. He was catching on fast.

'Just a little cameo role!'

'Wotcher, Dave,' Trig said, his face screwed up like a Pekinese. 'You dirty rat!'

'Hello, Trig,' Rodney replied.

Next up was the vicar. To start with, he seemed more concerned about Boycie and Marlene than his big break. 'I married the happy couple all those years ago, Derek. Of course, I hoped by now that the Good Lord would have blessed their union with an offspring or two. But if it's not to be . . .'

'I heard that, because of the precarious state of the world, Boycie and Marlene had decided against starting a family,' Rodney said.

The vicar looked puzzled. 'Oh, really?' he said. 'I

heard that Boycie was a Jaffa!' He paused. 'Is it true that you're making a film, Rodney?'

Rodney raised his eyes to the Great Producer in the Sky. 'Yes, that's right, vicar. We got an Arts Council grant.'

'I, er, I was talking to Derek earlier, and . . .'

'I'll phone you when we start shooting, vicar,' Rodney said.

'Gentlemen!' Boycie directed us to the viewing theatre upstairs. 'If you'd like to take your seats . . . The Boyce Video and Leisure Arts Company is proud to present the British premier of *Night Nurse*, from the novel by Enid Blyton.'

As the credits rolled I had a bad feeling. Rodders didn't seem too comfortable neither. I began to wonder what he and Mickey had been up to behind my back.

The movie started with a bird that looked the dead spit of Amanda taking off her uniform. As she did a bit of a wobble for the camera I heard Trig say: 'That must be special effects!'

'Where do they find these grotty flats to film in?' Mike asked, just as I thought I might have the answer. When Rodney suddenly appeared on screen, waving his arms at the cameraman and trying to hide in our kitchen, I knew for sure. I made a grab for him.

'It was nothing to do with me!' he squeaked. 'It was a Mickey Pearce production!'

'You wait till I get my hands on that Mickey Pearce!' I said. 'I'll take that camera and shove it half a mile up his nostril! Have you any idea what you're getting yourself into?'

'Well, I thought Boycie wouldn't be too pleased, someone muscling in on his business.'

'Boycie don't worry me, Rodney. It's his backers that are giving me grief. If the Driscoll Brothers reckon I'm copping location fees from their competition, I'll wind up starring as the horse's head in their remake of *The Godfather*!' I grabbed the video cassette. 'And to try and make sure your knees stay roughly where they are, I'm sticking this down the khazi!'

I was thinking of flogging Trotter Broadcasting to the Japanese when I overheard Rodney answer the phone the next morning.

'Hello?' he said. 'Oh, Mr Stevens, hi! Have you had time to read it? Good ... Well, what do you think? And be truthfully blunt with me ... yes ... aha! ... mmm. Well, that is very truthfully blunt, Mr Stevens. Yes, there are a lot of characters in it, but all vital to the theme. Yes, well, you see, I actually wanted to write a film that not only dealt with contemporary issues but also challenged some of the more widely held beliefs of modern youth.'

He paused for a moment before continuing. 'No, that is no problem, Mr Stevens. My brother Del knows where he can get a rhino . . .'

CHAPTER SEVEN

....

A Sense of Tradition

If there's one thing that separates your tycoon from your average plonker, it's a sense of tradition. What was the first present Alan Blond gave himself when he'd borrowed his

Believe in your product. Thomas Cook started up shop with the one bus, and he didn't even have a lifetime at the Peckham Business School behind him.

second billion? An English village. What did Bobby Murdoch do the very minute he got into satellite TV? Hire Angela Rippon. That's one of the reasons I've absolutely refused to move TITCO's HQ from Nelson Mandela House.

Like Prince Charles says, we've got to protect our heritage. That's why I secured Rodders a position a few years ago with a recently formed security company. They wanted a man with previous experience but, seeing as his last job was milk monitor, I had to doctor his CV. I managed to swing it for him in the end, though. I happened to know the guvnor rather well.

'What's this recently formed company called, Del?' Rodney asked.

'You wouldn't have heard of them,' I said. I wanted to play my cards close to my chest on this one for, well, security reasons.

'Try me. Come on, Del, let's have it!'

'It's called . . . er . . . Trotter Watch.'

Even Rodney saw through that one.

'Trotter Watch? It's you, ain't it? I'm working for you!'

Somehow I don't think he saw this as a great opportunity.

'Look, the way I see it, Rodney, crime's a growth industry. So I'm getting in now while the going's good. It's a nice regular job—uniform—good wages.'

I knew he'd change his mind as soon as he heard about the uniform.

'I used to be a security officer, you know, before the war,' announced TITCO's very own link with history.

'You mean someone actually trusted you with their property, Grandad?' I said. 'Stroll on. That's like trusting a piranha fish with your finger—or worse!'

The old fossil carried on regardless. 'Oh, yeah! It was a big warehouse over Kilburn way, stocked with everything from bedroom suites to kiddies' toys. There was a fella worked there, he used to arrive every morning in a big Wolseley car. He wore a camelhair overcoat and kid gloves and always carried a brand-new leather attaché case and used to smoke expensive cigars. Well, call it intuition if you like, but I was suspicious of him.'

'Why?'

'Well, he was only a sweeper-up! Anyhow, one night as he was leaving I stopped him and searched his attaché case. It was empty. But I *knew* something was up. I stopped him and searched his attaché case every night for a whole year. Then he left.'

'I wonder why?'

'I don't remember. I think he claimed someone was victimizing him. Didn't have unions in them days. Anyhow, a couple of weeks after he left the auditors came. Do you know what they discovered? We were missing three hundred and forty-eight attaché cases!'

'You mean you were actually searching the stolen gear?'

'Yeah. And I got done for it. Fingerprints.'

'Sit down,' I said to my fellow directors. 'I've got something very important to discuss with you. Rodney, you have to understand that this security job of yours is merely a tiny part of my immaculate scheme.'

'What immaculate scheme?'

'The tourist trade, Rodney. They're pouring into

London at the rate of about two thousand a day. Now I happen to know that, despite the fact that tourism's never been so high, the coach-party trade is falling off. And do you know why? No, I don't know, Del. Well, I'll tell you, Rodney. Because your average tourist is sick and tired of the Houses of Parliament, Buck House, the National Gallery—I mean, once you've seen one Rubens, you've seen the lot. And that is where a dynamic person like me steps in. You see, there is a more vibrant, more traditional London waiting out there to be discovered . . . Ethnic London!'

I know we hear a lot of chat about mobile phones and fax machines, pocket calculators and flash motors these days, but what the punters need is a link with the past. All except Rodney, that is. What he needs most is a link with the present.

They were staring at me in amazement.

'Yes!' I continued. 'Romantic places we've only heard about in fairy tales. The Lee Valley viaduct, the glory of Lower Edmonton at dusk, the excitement of a walkabout in Croydon.'

I handed Rodney one of the leaflets I'd had printed.

116

I'd a thousand done, in French, German, Japanese and Arabic.

'It's a well-known fact that at least ninety per cent of foreign tourists come from abroad, so we've got to speak the lingo, ain't we?'

'We?' Rodney said.

'Oh, French already. I like it, Rodney.'

'No, Del, I wasn't talking in French. I meant, what do you mean "we"?'

'Well, this is a family enterprise, ain't it? Grandad'll be selling the programmes, I'll be the courier, and you'll be driving the bus. It'll mean an extra wage.'

'I've already got a wage, Del!'

'But you can't live on what I'm paying you, can you!'

'I don't know, Del. What *are* you paying me?'

I thought it was time to move to the next item on the agenda.

'Look, Rodney, I did a deal with the coach garage. I provide them with a nightwatchm . . . a nocturnal security operative, and they provide me with an open-topped bus. See, that way no money changes hands—it saves all that paperwork and . . .'

'Income tax?'

He took the words right out of my mouth.

'Don't let me down, Rodney. A lot of thought and effort's gone into this. This morning Grandad was up at the crack of dawn distributing pamphlets in every hotel, boarding house and hostel he could find.'

We clearly stated on our leaflets that the departure time was nine o'clock. But there we were, eleven thirty and it wasn't exactly the first day of the Harrods sale. In fact, there was no sign of anybody.

'I told you, no one'll turn up,' Grandad said.

'Oh, yes, they will. Once the news spreads they'll be here in droves. I'm just worried whether a fifty-nine seater will be big enough. Perhaps I should have ordered three.'

'A tandem would be too big,' Grandad said.

That's what I like, optimism. When I got round to restructuring TITCO, some of the staff were going to find their names under the heading of Natural Wastage.

'I bet you not one single tourist arrives.'

I wasn't taking that without a fight. 'All right, I'll bet you fifty quid.'

'How much are you charging them for this tour?' Rodney asked.

'Seventeen quid.'

'Seventeen quid for a walkabout in Croydon?'

'That includes lunch,' I said. 'A selection of traditional British fare. A doner kebab, or something like that.'

'A doner kebab? For seventeen nicker I'd want Donna Summers.'

He's always been a tight little wad, Rodney. But these tourists wouldn't mind splashing out when they saw what they were getting for their money. I produced a couple of reproduction statues from a box. 'You watch them snap these souvenirs of Olde London up,' I said. 'They're a snip at five quid a go—almost alabaster, you know.'

'You're going to flog them models of a Roman statue now housed in the Louver gallery, Paris, as souvenirs of Olde London? It's the Venus de Milo, Del.'

'No, Rodders,' I explained patiently, 'it's Boadicea, ain't it?'

'Boadicea rode a chariot with swords sticking out from the wheels.'

'All right, she fell off. They won't know any better, Rodney.'

'You're just ripping them off, aren't you?'

I sometimes wondered if he was ever going to make the grade. '*Au contraire*, Rodney. The last thing I want to do is send them home tonight potless. I want to leave them with some money in their pockets. At least enough to give us a tip.'

'But, as a courier, what do you actually know about these obscure places you intend to drag them to?'

'Nothing. Which is about twice as much as *they* know. I'll bluff it, Rodders, give them a bit of spiel. If the questions get too awkward I'll pretend I can't understand their English. It'll be a doddle, you'll see. I mean, today I plan to take them out to Shoreditch and show them the house where Sherlock Holmes was born.'

'Sherlock Holmes was fictional.'

'Was he? Oh, well, I'll tell them the house was blown up in the war. Then I'll take them over North London, show them where Jack the Ripper was buried.'

'Nobody knows where he was buried.'

He was starting to catch on. 'Then they can't prove me wrong, can they?'

'But you're not telling them the truth, are you?'

'The truth? Oh, you're so naïve, Rodders.'

Grandad woke up and offered his six penn'orth. 'I'll tell you one truth that you won't earn a brass farthing out of. No one is going to turn up.'

'They will turn up. Take it from me. This time next year we'll be millionaires.' This was going to be the big one. I was going to become the Freddie Baker of the highway.

As night fell, I stood staring at the sign we had up by the bus. The passport to a different world! I just couldn't understand it. I'd planned it down to the last

detail. I mean, Grandad distributed a thousand leaflets – a thousand. You'd have thought that one punter, just one, would have been interested.

Still, as Mum used to say: 'It's better to know you've lost, than not to know you've won.' Dear old Mum. She used to say some bloody stupid things . . .

I went down the dust chute when I got back to Nelson Mandela House. I was about to chuck in the sign when I noticed the bins were even fuller than usual. They were chock-a-block with leaflets advertising something or other. Some poor sod must have dropped a bundle. There must have been close on a thousand of them there.

CHAPTER EIGHT

The Japanese Challenge

One way and another, the Western financial community has been a bit lairy of the Japanese way of doing business ever since Pearl Harbor. These days Harry Kiri and his mates are into everything from pocket calculators to the Tower of London. Now they've discovered a way to make motorbikes look like cars, even Reliant are worried.

They've come a long way on a few take-aways in the land of the rising yen, and there's a lesson in it for all of us. I've found myself interfacing frequently with the Orientals in the last decade. Don't get me wrong, I'm still very much a Ruby Murray sort of person — I'd plump for a couple of popadums, a Roland Gosh and a mutton vindaloo any day over a chicken chop suey, but I've got to admit the Japs know a thing or two when it comes to silicon chips. And when I closed a major refurbishment deal down the Golden Lotus a while back, I realized we had more in common with them than the boys on the River Kwai have led us to believe.

'So that's all kosher, Mr Chin?' I said, elbowing his cat off the serving counter as we settled terms.

'Yes,' he said inscrutably. 'Do you take Barclaycards?'

'Do *you*?' I asked. He smiled.

'My men will be here first thing tomorrow morning, Mr Chin. About eleven.'

He seemed a bit choked. 'Can you not start today?'

I explained that this was the anniversary of my late mother's passing from this immortal curl. Tradition had it that TITCO ceased trading on the global market for the day whilst Rodders and I went down the cemetery to tend her grave. I always turn a bit misty-eyed at the thought of the old girl's headstone. It's over seven feet tall with scrolls and cherubim and choirs of angels. It's a monument to fibreglass and probably tax-deductible if my financial people ever get round to filing the returns.

'Well, I must dash,' I said. 'Got to buy some flowers.'

'Yes. I'm very sorry . . .'

'Oh, it's no sweat. I get them cheap off a geezer in the market.' And with a cheery 'Syanora' I was gone.

When attempting to trace a path back to the roots of my financial genius, I often think of my mother. She was a wonderful woman. She had long blonde hair sometimes, and every night she used to sit at the bar of the Nag's Head—which was Peckham's answer to

the Stock Exchange even then. I can picture her now, simulated beaverskin coat across her shoulders, a rum and Pep in one hand, twenty Senior Service in the other. A real lady.

I was younger then, and didn't have much cash, but she would always send me over three or four light-and-bitters or a whisky if she was flush. Then about ten o'clock she'd shout across: 'Get off home to bed, Del Boy. School in the morning!' She was always concerned about our welfare.

In the big-business game, it all boils down to macho-economics.

God knows how she would have felt about young Rodney going out of his way to dodge yet another shot at the good life when I took him through the arithmetic on the Golden Lotus deal as we lay in the sunshine down the graveyard.

'The owner's in dead stuke,' I said. 'He's got the health inspector calling round, so he wants his kitchen painted—you know, tarted up a bit.'

'But how come I've got to paint it?'

'Grandad'll be there as well, Rodney, but you're the one with the GCE in Art! And it's a good earner. I'm charging him a hundred and fifty nicker!'

He wasn't having any, so I had to remind him of Mum's deathbed wish: 'She made me promise. "Del Boy," she said, "share everything you've got with

Rodney. Try to make him feel ... normal." And that's what I've always done, bruv. Half of everything I've got ... I mean, fair enough, I've got nothing just at the moment, but half of it's yours!'

'Do me a favour!' he said. 'You'd nick the hole out of my last Polo if I didn't keep my mouth closed!'

You only have to dip into the *FT* to see that your top earners are being accused of this sort of thing all the time. But it don't make it any easier to take.

'That hurts, Rodney,' I said. 'If I had any kind of wealth I'd give half of it to you like a shot!'

'Yeah? Say you had two Rolls-Royces . . .'

I was impressed. He'd taken on board one of the most fundamental theoretical lessons of the Peckham Business School.

'I'd give one to you.'

'You'd give me one of your Rolls-Royces?'

I nodded. 'I'd say: "Here you are, Rodney, here's a Rolls-Royce." I'd give you the one with the sun-roof.'

'If you had two million pounds, what would you do?'

I'd thought about that a lot so was able to answer him without hesitation: 'I'd give you the second million, wouldn't I?'

'Really?'

He looked like he was going to get straight on the dog and call our legal people.

'Yes,' I said. 'In cash.'

He paused. Then his face got that sly look that usually means it's my round.

'What would you do if you had two of them deep-sea diver's watches?'

'Don't take bloody liberties with me, Rodney,' I said, indicating that the board meeting was at an end. 'You know I've got two of them deep-sea diver's watches!'

'That's the real Del coming out!'

'All right. I'll give you one of my deep-sea diver's watches!'

'No!' he said, getting back on his high horse. 'I've got to draw the line somewhere. I'm fed up with you and your bribery and emotional blackmail every time you want me to do the dirty work. It's a point of principle. You might as well get it straight. I am *not* painting that kitchen tomorrow, I'm not painting it in a thousand years. No way, my son!'

I realized it was time to offer what we in management call an inducement.

'I'll give you a lend of my dirty books . . .'

'All right then,' he said.

Lovely jubbly.

The first thing Rodney did on arrival at the Golden Lotus was to let the cat out.

'Well, that's going to please Mr Chin, ain't it?' I said.

'Was it his pet?'

I shook my head. Unlike Rodney, my years of conducting business with foreigners has left me with some considerable knowledge of their culture.

'Put it this way,' I said. 'If they don't manage to catch it, number thirty-nine's off the menu.'

It's possible that the mog may just have had a more highly developed sense of personal hygiene than Mr Chin. When I switched the lights on in the kitchen I was gobsmacked. It looked like an explosion in a dripping factory. There was rotting meat and veg wall to wall.

'Nice little kitchen, ain't it?' I said.

I sensed from the look on Rodney's face that he was not about to second the motion.

'Nice little kitchen? It's the pits, Del Boy, the bloody pits! It looks like an explosion in a dripping factory!'

'It's a working kitchen, Rodney,' I explained patiently. 'You can't help a bit of fat splashing out of the pan every now and then.'

'What period we going to decorate it in, Del? Early bubonic?'

I was just wondering whether inoculations was a legitimate business expense when Grandad came in with his portable TV. I could see he was keen to get stuck in.

'Is this the kitchen then?' he asked.

'No,' I said. 'This is the master bedroom, you wally! Now listen, you could be out of here in a

couple of days if you don't do silly things like stopping for lunch.'

Rodney looked at the remains of last month's stir-fried prawn balls on the draining board. 'Lunch ain't my top priority right now, Del. Let's get it over and done with then. What colour are we going for? These soppy little tins of paint ain't got no labels on them!'

Time and emotion: the most essential lesson to be learnt at the Peckham Business School. (Rodney was about as good at grasping that principle as Michael Angelo.) In a crowded schedule one of the most vital verdicts of the School is never take a call until you are ready.

'I know. The owner bought them cheap. He got well taken on—it's a load of rubbish.'

'You can say that again. Where did he get them from?'

'Me,' I said.

'*You?* Is this nicked, Del? I'm not doing this if they're nicked!'

Not for the first time, I wondered if I was ever going to get Rodney past the first fence in the entreprunerial stakes.

'It's not nicked, Rodney! It's bankrupt stock. I

129

bought a couple of gross as a job lot. Trust me, will you? Trust me.'

Mr Chin appeared as we were just trying to open the first paint tin to see what colour it was.

'Ah, good morning, Mr Chin,' I said, bowing inscrutably. 'Well, my men are here as promised. And may I say that these two are the very best in the business— the *crème de la menthe* of the decorating world. Don't worry about a thing, Mr Chin. In fact, chin up, Mr Chin, as we say in this country!'

'Have you decided what colour the walls will be?' he said.

Rodney was still going the best of three falls with the lid, so this item was a bit too early on the agenda for my liking.

'Colour?' I said. 'Oh, but of course. We don't leave important decisions like that until the last minute ... Er, do we, Rodney? Now ... Well, what I thought, Mr Chin, is—well, you may not like the colour I've chosen, but I somehow think you will. What, in fact, our panel of experts has decided on—and feel free to shoot me down in flames if you wish, is—'

That lid was coming away slower than a Sinclair C5 from the traffic lights.

'—so, the thing is with these particular walls—'

'Blue,' he said. 'I like blue.'

'Why, *jeux sans frontières*, that's exactly how I saw it, didn't I, Rodney? I thought, why don't we do it in a subtle shade of blue?'

'What shade of blue?'

'Yellow,' Rodney said as the lid suddenly skidded across the worktop and the contents of the mystery tin were finally revealed.

'But then I changed my mind, Mr Chin,' I said. 'I thought, no, blue's just not right. It's the Golden Locust we're talking about, so it's got to be gold!'

'It's yellow,' Rodney said.

'It's gold,' I said. 'What's the matter with you, illiterate or something?'

Fortunately, my combination of forceful negotiation and body language won the day.

Call me old-fashioned or sentimental, but I'm a readies man.

'Well, I'll leave it to you, Mr Trotter,' Mr Chin said. 'As long as my kitchen is cleaned up before the health inspector calls.'

'How do you know the health inspector's calling?' Rodney asked. 'I didn't think they warned you.'

'I had a telephone call from a man, he would not give his name, but he tells me: "Get your kitchen painted or you be in big trouble, John."'

Rodney's brow creased. 'John?'

'Yeah,' I said. 'John. Somebody up there likes him.'

'I *wonder* who that anonymous caller could have been, Del?'

I hate it when Rodney starts to get all sartorial.

'Well, I think I'll take this opportunity to say chow main and let these men get on with their work, Mr Chin.'

''Ere, Del,' Grandad said as I escorted our Oriental client to the door, 'do you think this anonymous person is likely to phone any other Chinese restaurants and tell them to get their kitchens painted?'

'Why? Your business diary starting to fill up, Grandad?' I asked. 'Oh, Rodney, don't forget to water that lot down a bit—the plaster's none too clever. A little dab'll do you.'

'What about all this grease, Del Boy? You arranged for anyone to clean it up?'

'Of course I have, Grandad,' I said. 'Do you think I'm a cowboy or something? There's a tin of Ajax and a rubber glove in that bucket. Go easy on the Ajax, won't you?'

Urgent business elsewhere kept me off-site for a couple of days, so unfortunately I only made it back to Mr Chin's HQ half an hour after the lads had finished the job. I picked up the hundred and fifty, handed Grandad thirty-five and Rodney forty and a deep-sea diver's watch.

'Don't get that wet, Rodders,' I advised him.

When we got back to the office Trigger was waiting with another consignment of paint.

'All right, Del Boy?' he said to me.

'Hello, Dave,' he said to Rodney. 'Got a watch?'

'What you up to, Trig?' I asked.

'I got some more of that paint. Interested?'

'Yeah, I'll take it off your hands. Same price or lower?'

'I won't be getting any more of this for a spell, Del. I'm laying low. We almost got caught the other night.'

Rodders stopped trying to get his watch to work. 'What do you mean, you almost got caught?'

'The railway police, Dave,' Trig said. 'See, me and Monkey Harris get this paint from a storage shed down at Clapham Junction.'

Rodney turned on me. 'You swore to me it wasn't nicked! You said it was bankrupt stock!'

'Well, it's British Rail. Same thing, ain't it?'

Rodney shook his head. 'Knocked off railway paint, eh? I bet Mr Chin would be pleased to know that he's just had his kitchen decorated in Inter-City yellow.'

'I prefer to call it Awayday gold,' I said.

'This ain't the stuff they paint trains with,' Trig said. 'They use this for painting the signs in tunnels.'

Rodney was still out of his depth. 'It doesn't matter what they use it for, Trig. It's knocked off. That means it's illegal.'

I had to put him right. 'It's for the good of the country, Rodders.'

'Good of the country? How can nicking off British Rail be good for Britain?'

I sighed. Rodney kills me sometimes. He's got a GCE in Maths and yet he acts like a congenital tit in a trance.

'I'll tell you why it's good for Britain,' I said. 'British Rail will have to hire more security guards to protect this paint, thus lowering the unemployment figures, plus their insurance company will need more people to process British Rail's claims, which means redundant insurance clerks will be snatched from the dole queues and given back their dignity. Now these people may well celebrate their good fortune by buying a new Reliant and taking the wife and kids on a touring holiday round Britain. This will result in a much needed boost for our ailing car industry, higher revenue for North Sea oil and the injection of cash into seaside resorts and other depressed areas. On the other hand, they may decide to holiday abroad, thus forcing foreign hoteliers, bar-owners and restauranteurs to order more British beer, food and goods, which will in turn help our export drive and result in a balance-of-payments surplus. Soon we'll be a rich and successful nation again, unemployment will be a thing of the past, the starving shall be fed, the homeless homed. Right?'

Rodney was open-mouthed with admiration.

After several minutes of deep concentration, he spoke: 'Del, this watch is broke.'

''Course it's not,' I said. 'You just don't know how to use it properly. Look, it tells you the time in all the world's major capitals!'

'Well, London's not on the map as far as this is concerned. All it tells me is that it's permanently chucking-out time in Peking and I'm low on oxygen.'

'Use your loaf, Rodders,' I said. 'When we start trading on the Japanese Stock Market and go for business dinners down the Ninja, it'll be invaluable!'

Grandad was so struck by my vision of the future that he chose that exact moment to come out of a coma.

'Tunnels!'

This caught us all a bit by surprise.

'Trigger said tunnels. He said they use that stuff to paint signs in tunnels. Well, how can you see a sign in a tunnel? It's pitch black, ain't it?'

'No,' said Trig. 'It's luminous paint . . .'

The phone started to ring and I started to have one of my little preconditions.

'I'm not in, Grandad,' I said.

'Oh, hello, Mr Chin,' Grandad said. 'No, Del's gone out . . . I'm not sure. Where you gone to, Del?'

'You daft old goat,' I said, reaching for the dog. I

took a deep breath. 'Hello, Mr Chin, how's things with you?'

'Don't you hello Mr Chin me!' he said. 'What you done to my walls?'

'Glowing, are they, Mr Chin? Great, ain't it? It's er, this new energy-saving paint we use. Yes, it's designed to cut down on the old electricity bill. I get it from a contact in . . . um . . . Stockholm. The Norwegians lead the world in paint technology . . .'

We talked specifications for some minutes and then I explained I had our Dubai office on the other line.

'Does he want his money back, Del?' Rodney asked.

'No,' I said. 'He wants you to go back and do his living-room out in it. I'll have that other box after all, Trig.'

As I was counting out the readies I suddenly went cold. I'd given Mum's monument a couple of coats the day before to brighten it up. It was going to be a beacon for every acid-head and born-again plonker in Southern England.

CHAPTER NINE

Cleaning Up

Rodney has been getting in right lumber about the ozone layer recently. To start with I thought he was complaining about the state of the TITCO executive khazi again. We've been having trouble ever since the wallies from the council put our extractor fan in the wrong way round. But no. He's rescued his Steve Bilko tee-shirt from the shoe-cleaning tin and been campaigning down the Nag's Head to save the Amazon Rainforest.

I'd have thought the Amazons would be dead chuffed with a climate a bit more like Majorca, but there you go. Apparently the ecosystem's in stuke and Anita Roddick and a limo-full of rock stars are trying to sort it out. I used to buy all her singles, so I said I'd do what I could.

The point of all this is: you don't have to be environmentally unfriendly to be a millionaire these days. In fact, only last week Boycie fitted me up with one of them new catatonic converters for the van. It fell off the back of a SAAB.

I draw the line at chucking my sheepskin jacket

into one of them skips in Trafalgar Square, but as a bit of a pioneer in the recycling game I think I'm already doing my bit for terra cotta, and I'm really cleaning up. Whether we're talking suntan lotion or Chippendale teapots, Ethiopian mink or digital Georgian clocks, I've been recycling gear for years.

To give you a for instance, Rodney was hardly out of short trousers when I took on a consignment of Old English vinyl briefcases from Trig.

The day started like any other. Grandad and Rodney were in a breakfast meeting as I put the finishing touches on some power dressing. I checked out the effect in the mirror.

'Oh, *s'il vous plaît*, what an enigma,' I said. 'I get better looking every day. I can't wait until tomorrow.' I took a deep breath and felt a sharp pain in the ribs. I put it down to the old executive stress.

'Come on, Rodney,' I said. 'Shake a leg. We've got a meeting at twelve. What are you doing?'

He'd finished his pizza and was scribbling furiously on the back of an envelope.

'Our accounts.'

My blood ran cold.

'You see what I mean, Grandad?' I said, grabbing the envelope. 'A lot of people said I was a right dipstick to make my brother a partner in the business, but this goes to prove how bloody right they were. You dozy twonk, Rodney, this is *prima facie* evidence!

If the tax man saw this he'd put us away for three years!'

Rodney was unmoved.

'Don't worry, Del. If the tax man drops round, I'll eat that. It's the only way I can keep a check on you. You're cheating me in some way. I just can't figure out how.'

'*Cheating you?*' I felt that sharp pain in the ribs again. 'Hang on, what's that rumbling noise?'

'I didn't hear nothing.'

'It's all right,' I said. 'I think it was Mum turning in her grave.'

'Don't start that again! It's obvious you're stitching me up. You have three or four changes of clothes a day. Me? I've got one suit and that came from the Almost New shop. It gets embarrassing sometimes.'

Don't I know it. Rodders used to be a little scruff when he was younger. Now he's a big scruff. In the corporate-image race, he still ain't even got to the starting grid. It got so embarrassing I had to take his name off the TITCO letterhead, GCEs or no GCEs.

'What sort of bloke do you think I am?' I said. 'Cheat my own brother? I've told you before and I'll tell you again: we split everything down the middle, sixty/forty!'

'Well, explain this to me, Del. How do we manage to pay the rent, light and gas in this flat? Take last week alone. We went to the auction and bid for a gross of disposable lighters, a space invaders game, two facial saunas, five water-damaged sleeping bags and a moon-roof for a Peugeot. Then we swopped the lot for a van-load of one-legged turkeys!'

I wondered whether Jimmy Goldfield's brother gave him this kind of grief.

'They were not one-legged turkeys. They were *damaged* turkeys.'

'Well, how many legs did they have?'

'I'm not in the mood for trick questions,' I said, glancing down at his accounts. 'Here, you haven't put down VAT.'

'We don't pay VAT.'

I sighed. 'But we collect it, Rodney. We collect it.'

He gave me one of his poncey looks. I realized I was going to have to hit him with a sharpish lecture on comparative economics before we went down the Nag's.

'Look,' I said, 'fair enough, we don't pay any VAT, Income Tax or National Insurance. But, on the other hand, we don't claim any dole money, social security or supplementary benefit. The Government don't give us nothing and we don't give the Government nothing. So what are you complaining about?'

'I'm twenty-three and I'd like to think that I had some kind of a career.'

'But you're self-unemployed, Rodney,' I pointed out. 'That's a career ain't it?'

'What, selling hankies from a suitcase in Oxford Street? I want something better than that, Del!'

As any graduate of the Peckham Business School will tell you, the secret of good labour relations is to act swiftly and decisively. 'All right, from now on you can do Regent Street. Come on.'

Unfortunately, the fresh air didn't do Rodney any good at all. He was still like a tit in a trance when we convened at the Nag's.

If you're going to enjoy any success in the import–export game, you've got to think time zones. Just as your average wage-slave is mixing himself a cup of cocoa and thinking of bed, us yuppies are settling down with the mobile phone to do some business in the global marketplace. While you're power-breakfasting in Peckham, your Sydney tycoon's about ready for a kip. It's a miracle they get anything done.

'Do you realize, Del, that we've always had something missing in our lives? First we were motherless, then we were fatherless, and now we're flogging one-legged turkeys from a three-wheeled van.'

'Little acorns!' I said.

'You got one of them missing as well, Del?'

Joyce came over to take our order. She was my kind of girl, Joyce. Peckham's answer to Dolly Parton and everything on the counter.

'*Bonjour*, Joyce,' said I. 'We'll have two halves of your finest low-carbohydrate lager, *danke schön*!'

'Do you want it in glasses?' she said.

'Yeah, otherwise it all dribbles through your fingers!'

'I meant did you want it in glasses or jugs, Del?' She was well amused.

I gave her one of my upraising looks and wondered about going for the jugs.

'As long as it's served by your fair hands, Joyce, we'd drink it out of Yvonne Goolagong's old tennis boots.'

Joyce headed for the till.

'Charm like laser beams, Rodney,' I said. 'Knocks them bandy.'

'It's your ready wit and three-wheeled van that blows their minds,' he agreed.

'Yeah, I am a bit full of the *bel esprit*. I like Joycie. I mean, fair enough, she's a bit of an old dog, but there again, I like old dogs. You know where you stand with them. They never ask if you remember their name in the morning, and they'll always lend you a nicker for petrol.'

I breathed deeply of the atmosphere. Aside from

Rodney's plimsoles there was the scent of excitement, of infinite possibilities.

'I love this life, Rodders,' I continued. 'I mean in our game you can go out in the morning with fifty pence in your pocket . . .'

'And come home at night skint,' he said.

'Exactly!'

When our drinks arrived, Rodney took a sip and then concentrated hard on his fingernails.

'I'm thinking of getting a job, Del . . .'

'A *job*?'

'I've got GCEs and I took a year's course at that art college in Basingstoke . . .'

'Yes, Rodders, you took a year's course, but you got expelled after three weeks for being zonked out on your bed with some Chinese tart!'

'She was not a Chinese tart!'

'Chinese, Japanese—it's all the same to me.'

I leant closer to him. Every once in a while a chief executive owes it to his staff to give them an accurate assessment of their future. I realized that time had come.

'So what would you say at your interview, Rodney? "Oh, yes, sir, I've got qualifications and experience. I've got two O-levels, an eighteen-month suspended sentence and I know a good joint when I puff one?" Your feet won't touch, bruv! You see, at the grand old age of twenty-three you are a social leper. Society has placed you in the darkest corner of its deepest cellar to gather moss and be forgotten about. Still, never mind, eh? *Viva la France*. No need to get depressed. This time next year we'll be millionaires!'

I gave him an encouraging smile and looked up to see Trigger approaching for our appointment. He'd taken a bit of trouble with his rig. His grubby old jeans, shortie Wellingtons and donkey jacket were offset very nicely by a spanking new vinyl briefcase.

'All right, Trigger?' I said. 'You know my brother, don't you?'

''Course I do.' He nodded at Rodney. 'How you going, Dave?'

Some people think he's called Trigger because he carries a gun. In fact it's because he looks like a horse. I tried to remember if I'd ever seen his brain break into a canter.

We went over to a side table as Rodney took care of another round. 'He's a clever kid, my brother,' I said. 'No doubt about it. Two GCEs in Maths and Art, and you should see him write a letter. The words he uses!'

Trig was impressed. 'Long ones?'

'Long?' I said. 'Rodney knows more about syllables than Mr Kipling knows about cakes! Anyway, Trig, what you selling?'

'This!' He pointed to the briefcase. 'I've got twenty-five all told. The others are in the car. I thought I wouldn't wrap it up. Parcels attract a lot of attention these days. Best to carry it openly then it don't look conspicuous!'

'Good thinking,' I said. 'And it goes perfect with your slingback wellies and off-the-shoulder donkey jacket. You look like an executive hod-carrier!'

I examined the merchandise as Rodney came over with the drinks.

'What do you reckon, Rodders? They're a bit infra dig, eh?'

'It's plastic.'

'Plastic?' I gave it a

Make a note in the Filofax to go and open an account at the bottle bank.

sniff. A good businessman always follows his nose. 'No, that's Old English vinyl. Combination locks, dinky little handle—we might be able to punt them round the squash clubs.'

'I don't think we should have anything to do with them,' he said. 'The police are probably looking for them right now.'

I looked at Trigger. 'Tell me the truth, Trig. Are the police on the trail of these things?'

He reached across, grabbed the case and put it under the table. 'No, they're not, Del. And that's the truth.'

'Leave them, Del,' Rodney said. 'Come on, we're partners. At least respect my opinion.'

'All right, Rodney. I respect your opinion,' I said. 'How much, Trig?'

'To you, Del Boy, seventeen pounds each!'

It wasn't exactly sale of the century. I decided to lay on some negotiating magic.

'You know what happened to the real Trigger, don't you? Roy Rogers had him stuffed.'

'All right, fourteen.'

I shook my head. 'Five.'

'Ten.'

Rodney's head was going from side to side like he was watching Wimbledon.

'Nine,' I said.

'Eight,' Trigger said.

'Done,' I said.

Trigger beamed. 'That's the way to do business, Dave!'

I brought out the old slimline executive calculator.

'Right, eight times twenty-five equals a hundred and seventy-five.' I started counting off the wad.

'Two hundred,' Rodney said, his mouth several seconds ahead of his brain.

'What?' I said. 'No, no—the calculator definitely says a hundred and seventy-five, Rodney.'

'Yeah,' Trig said, 'but *he*'s got GCEs in Maths and Art!'

'So what does that prove, he can paint by numbers? The calculator says a hundred and seventy-five

and you can't argue with technology, now can you?'

'Give me the calculator, Del,' Rodney said.

'Are you sure you don't have another meeting to go to?'

There was no stopping him. As I watched his fingers dance over the keyboard I thought that if he ever decided to play on my team we'd be a lot closer to that first million.

'Eight times twenty-five, Del. Equals? Two hundred, see!'

'Well, well, well,' I said. 'I must have got one of my fingers stuck on the button.'

Rodney smiled and flexed his knuckles. 'Pianist's fingers, Del.'

I flexed mine as I counted off another twenty-five contributions to overhead.

'You want to look after those pianist's fingers, Rodney,' I said. 'They break very easily.'

Like every successful mogul, I've never been a nine-to-five man.

And so it was that at half eight that evening the nerve centre of the TITCO empire was still humming. Grandad was watching *Paddington Bear* on the video, Rodney was unwrapping a take-away cheeseburger, and I was on the dog to Spiros down the Lord Byron Doner Inn. The briefcase boxes were on display in the middle of the stockroom.

'You've got to see them to believe them, Spiros! What? I'm not sure . . .'

I put my hand over the mouthpiece and asked Grandad to check where they were made.

'It don't say,' he said. 'There's some Chinese writing on them, though.'

'It don't actually give the maker's name, Spiros,' I continued. 'There again, the best ones never do!'

'How's it going?' Rodney said helpfully.

Grandad tore himself momentarily away from Paddington. 'That's about the fifteenth.'

'Briefcase he's sold?'

'No, phone call he's made.'

'Get in while the going's good, Spiros,' I said. 'I've only got twenty-five of them left! How many shall I put you down for?'

'None,' he said.

Rodney raised an eyebrow as I put down the phone.

'He could only pay by cheque,' I said.

'I told you the best thing to do with them cases, didn't I? Chuck them in the river!'

'Chuck them in the river? That's our profit you're talking about. What do you think this is, a nationalized industry?'

I thumbed through my little black Filofax and spotted the name of the bloke who owns the stationer's down the high road.

'Dougie Sadler, Rodders. He's our man!'

'You're a tryer, ain't you?' Grandad said, beaming with pride. 'Your Dad always said one day you'd reach the top. There again, he used to say the same about Millwall . . .'

I was back on the mobile. 'Dougie?' I said. 'Del Boy here. How's your luck, pal? Family? Soooper! Listen, Doug, I'm phoning about some briefcases . . . Yeah? What a choker!' Incredible coincidence. He'd had twenty-five briefcases nicked from his shop the previous week. 'No, Doug, I wasn't trying to buy some, I've got a contact on the Stock Exchange, see. Just out of interest, Dougie, baby, how much were you selling them for? What do you mean, they were rejects?'

I sat and stared for a while at the pile of boxes. *Joy de vivre!* This was what it must have been like on Wall Street during the Great Bash. I tightened my Gordon Gekko braces. I was sitting on a bare market and it was going to be a rough ride.

'All right,' Rodney said. 'So what's wrong with them?'

'Open one.'

He fiddled with the locks.

'What's the combination?'

'No sod knows. Cock-up at the factory. They locked the paperwork inside the cases . . .'

'Oh, beautiful, Del Boy! You've bought twenty-five executive briefcases that can only be opened by professional safecrackers. This makes the one-legged turkey deal look shrewd!'

'That's the way I'm made, Rodney,' I explained. 'Crash in and take the consequences! He who dares wins! The French have a word for people like me!'

Marks and Spencer started off with a barrow. They used to dream about buying a three-wheeled van.

'The English have got a couple of good ones as well,' he said, missing the point as usual. 'Next time, perhaps you'll pay a bit more attention to your financial adviser.'

I couldn't believe it. 'Financial adviser? *Bonjour Trieste*. You're a regular Nigel Dawson, Rodney! Today I'd just about clinched a deal to buy those briefcases for a hundred and seventy-five pounds when my financial adviser stuck his nose in and advised me to pay *two* hundred for them. Then having paid *two* hundred, my financial adviser advised me to chuck the bleeding lot in the river! With financial advisers like that, who needs a recession?'

The rest of this Extraordinary General Meeting of the board of TITCO went unminuted. I do remember, though, that it showed signs of getting a bit personal.

'I don't understand you, Rodney,' I said at one point. 'Sometimes I hesitate to tell people you're my brother!'

'I always pretend I'm your social worker.'

He said it was my fault he'd been the only sixth-former in his grammar school who wore short trousers (I got them cheap) and that if I'd organized the Last Supper it would have been a take-away. Then he told me he was going to prove he was going to survive on his own in the wild, borrowed two fivers and left to see that Chinese tart in Hong Kong. I had half a mind to tell him to take Trig's briefcases with him. He could have dropped them back at the factory.

'I think he's very much like you, Grandad,' I said after he'd gone.

'What? Dignified in defeat?'

'No, a ponce.'

He made it as far as the Shangri La doss house in Stoke Newington, where he shared a room with a couple of cholera cultures. He came back six days later, claiming to miss the view from Nelson Mandela House. It didn't wash. Neither had he.

I'd thought a lot about those briefcases in Rodney's absence, though. I'd thought about trying to shift them through this bric-à-brac shop I knew. Then I'd thought about all them little vinyls being cruelly slaughtered for their hides just so we yuppies could be a bit ostentatious at business meetings.

Wiping the tears from my eyes, I'd chucked all twenty-five of the bleeders into the river and stood watching for a moment as they floated out to sea.

CHAPTER TEN

Going Offshore

I've always been one of them blokes who's accepted anywhere, whether it's drinking lager with the market boys down Nine Elms or sipping Pimm's fruit cup at the Hendon Regatta.

No matter what Sir John Harvey-Oswald says, there are times when it's better to lose thruppence than a fiver.

Since the dawn of timeshares, us Trotters have always been looking for new frontiers to cross, new Nothing to Declare channels to whistle down. It's in the blood. Uncle Albert joined the Navy and spent a lot of World War Two in a storage depot in the Isle of Wight. Dad left home with little more than my savings, my three-quarter-length suede, Rodney's piggy bank and my sixteenth birthday cake. Even Grandad managed to tear himself away from his armchair in his youth to sell Lee Enfields that were past their sell-by dates to both sides in the Spanish Civil War.

TITCO made its mark behind the Iron Curtain

long before they ripped down the Berlin Wall and turned it into an earner. We're the market leader in Albanian watches, Turkish raincoats, Bulgarian three-piece suits, that sort of thing.

As 1995 approaches we're well poised to enter Europe. After all, it's just a short hike from Nelson Mandela House to the Old Kent Road; you're on Shooter's Hill in no time and less than five hours later: *à fait accomplan*! The three-wheeled van's stashed below and you're getting a Cointreau and Diet Pepsi down you on the ferry—unless Rodney's buying and you have to make do with a swift half of Barbican and an early night.

The fact is, sooner or later every serious punter knows he's going to have to move offshore. Only yesterday Danny Driscoll was down the Nag's telling me he thought Peckham was probably not big enough for the both of us. That set me thinking. My first idea was Australia. My old mucker Alan Blond did all right down there, and he was only a sign painter from Catford. Mind you, Catford probably seems pretty cushty to him now.

'Blondie's in deep stuke,' I said to Rodney when we last met to review the contents of the *Financial Times*. 'His empire's in ruins. Look at the Don Jones index. His name's not even mentioned! That's always a bad sign. This time next year he'll know more about hock than a German wine-taster.'

Rodney opened his mouth and closed it a couple of times. He was either dead impressed or pretending to be a goldfish.

'Let's hope it never happens to us, Rodders,' I said. 'If my funds was castrated like that, I'd do an Arthur.'

Rodney was puzzled. 'A J. Arthur?'

I smiled at his ignorance. 'No, my son. An Arthur Scargill.'

Watching Blondie getting tucked up something chronic reminds me of the time my old partner Jumbo Mills tried to persuade me to shift the TITCO head office Down Under. He'd flown all the way from Sydney to the saloon bar of the Nag's Head to finalize the deal.

I was having a leisurely Tia Maria and Lucozade with Rodney and Uncle Albert when I copped Jumbo. He had a face like a crocodile handbag, an accent that had been hit by a frying-pan and a syrup like Jimmy Savile's hearth rug. Boycie was ordering up a business lunch as he tried to interest him in a couple of slightly used motors.

'Put it on my account, Michael,' Boycie said to the landlord.

'What account?' Mike said.

'See what I mean, Jumbo?' Boycie laughed. 'The old place ain't lost its sense of humour!'

'Well, *I* wouldn't laugh if a barman made a berk out of me!'

Jumbo had always managed to play hookey from charm school. I went over before Mike could reach over and rearrange his headgear. He never did like to be called barman.

'Jumbo bloody Mills,' I greeted him. 'Who let you back in the country?'

'Oh, look at this! Talk about the bad penny! Del Boy, how are you, mate?'

Boycie welcomed me to their table: 'Jumbo and I are having a business meeting, Derek. It's all rather confidential.'

'I've got no secrets from Del,' Jumbo said. 'Me and him were partners back in the sixties.'

I nodded. 'We used to run a fish stall outside the pub here. Those were the days, eh?'

I asked him how long he was back for.

'Just a week or so. I'm here to do this deal with Boycie and take in a bit of sightseeing, though I wish I hadn't bothered. This country's like a cess-pit!'

I knew the view from Nelson Mandela House was nothing to write home about, but I wasn't about to sit there and listen to a bleeding imitation Aussie sound off about this septic isle.

Boycie, on the other hand, wasn't prepared to turn this into a deal-breaker. 'You're right there, Jumbo!' he said.

'Cess-pit?' I said. 'What do you mean, a cess-pit?'

'You could find cleaner places in an Abbo's armpit!' Jumbo roared.

Boycie was laughing so hard I thought he'd lose his moustache up his nose.

'I tell you what, Jumbo,' I said. 'You can't tell that's a wig!'

Jumbo went very still. 'That's because it's not a wig.'

'Do me a favour! You used to have curly hair! That's a syrup!'

'Course it ain't a syrup!' Boycie said, trying to stop his quarterly figures taking a nose-dive.

I put a couple of notes on the table. 'I've got a tenner says that is a syrup.'

Boycie followed suit. 'I've got a tenner says it ain't!'

'Boycie,' I said, 'that is what we graduates of the Peckham Business School refer to as a loss leader.'

I had the whole score in my pocket in half the time it took to whip Jumbo's wig off his bonce.

'Thank you very much,' I said.

Jumbo didn't see the funny side at all. For a moment I thought his head was going to explode.

'What the flaming hell do you think you're playing at?'

Boycie was a bit shaken and all. 'I don't believe you sometimes, Del. I'm trying to clinch a deal here, and you've nicked my client's wig!'

'But it was a bet,' I said reasonably. 'You do

understand, don't you, Jumbo?'

'No, I bloody well don't!' he bleated, trying to reinstate his rug. Finally he gave up and put it in his pocket. 'Anyway, this is just a temporary condition. The doctors have said that my own hair will grow back eventually!'

'Is that a fact, Jumbo?' I said. 'You must remind me to buy some shares in your barber's.'

'He seems a nasty piece of work,' Uncle Albert said when I went back to the bar.

I shook my head and smiled. 'No, that's just the way he talks. Jumbo's all right. He's got a heart of gold and he's as straight as a dye!'

The man himself came by a moment or two later, on the way to the gents'.

'Oi, Jumbo,' I said, nodding towards Rodney. 'Do you remember my horrible little kid brother? Funny haircut and all snot and Marmite?'

'Yeah, I remember,' he said. 'You ain't changed a bit, Rodney.'

Rodders wasn't too sure whether to take that as a compliment.

'This is Jumbo Mills,' I said. 'Remember him?'

'No.'

'Well, you were just a sprog when he emigrated to Australia. Done very well for himself too.'

'You can say that again, mate,' Jumbo said. 'Best thing I ever did was get out of this dump! Now I'm a major shareholder in an office-cleaning company and a chain of fast-food restaurants, and I'm just going into the automobile trade. Last year I bought a unit overlooking Sydney Harbour. Half a million dollars! Architect-designed interior, right down to the mirrored ceiling in the bedroom . . .'

'Mirrored ceiling!' I said.

'Ooh! Kinky!' Rodney said.

I got the feeling the mirrored ceiling was one thing Jumbo's brain wished his mouth had kept a secret.

'It's purely decorational! I mean, I don't use it for anything like . . . well, like *that* . . .'

'Well, you wouldn't use it for combing your hair, would you?' Albert said.

Jumbo's suntan turned the colour of ripe tomato.

'You think I'm bald, don't you?'

'It had crossed my mind,' Rodney said.

'Well, I'm not!'

'That's a hell of a parting you've got there, my son!' Albert said.

'I mean I'm not *naturally* bald!'

Rodney was flabbergasted. 'You mean you *pay* someone to do that?'

'He's only winding you up, Jumbo,' I said.

He put his proposition to me later that evening. I chose a rollneck and sheepskin combo for the occasion, to make him feel at home. Then I added a chunky bracelet and a couple of medallions for luck. It wasn't what we in the financial community call highly geared, but it would have got Sir Ralph Heartburn's vote.

When we arrived at the Nag's I decided to kick off with a banana Daktari and an Australian lager for Jumbo.

Mike was still a bit out of sorts. 'I only sell British lager,' he said. 'Kronenburg, Hofmeister, things like that.'

We settled for one of them.

Jumbo admired my threads.

'How's that first million coming along?' he said. I grinned and rattled my medallions. 'You should come with me, mate. You're wasted here. This country's finished. It's old and decrepit!'

'Yeah?' I said. 'Well, it's still my country, so stop having a pop at it!'

'Hey, come on, mate. I didn't mean to offend you. I'm just trying to point out a few facts . . .' He took a pull on his lager before going on. 'Do you remember when our business broke up and I decided to emigrate?'

'We went into liquidation,' I said. 'It was one of them really hot days and all the ice melted on the stall.'

'If it weren't for you, Del, I'd have gone to Australia potless. You gave me your last two hundred pounds.'

'I told you to forget it.'

'Well, I never did, mate. Even when times were hard I used to lay in bed at night and think to myself: one day I'm going to pay Del back, with interest! And now I am. I want us to reform our old partnership!'

'What?' I said. 'Get another fish stall?'

'No! I'm setting up a company to import prestige European cars—Rollers, Mercs, that sort of thing. Del, I want you to come to Oz to front the business, deal with the public, give them the old razzamatazz like you used to!'

I had to admit this vacancy sounded as though it had my name written all over it.

'I've got the money, I've got the site and now, thanks to my little deal with Boycie, I've got the cars. All I need is you!'

Like many men of vision operating at the sharp end of the financial pencil, I've never restricted my activities to one manor. Import– export is very much a people game, and many's the club that's been brought to its knees by the transfer of a star player.

It wasn't the first time Del Trotter had been head-hunted. The Driscoll brothers had tried it a number of times. So had that geezer from Parkhurst whose old lady had shacked up for a while with Rodney. But I'd always stood firm.

'Australia,' I said. 'It ain't half a long way away . . .'

'Del, they'd love you over there. They've got no class. I mean, no class structure. They've got money instead. Derek, stand on me. This time next year you'll be that millionaire!'

'But I've got family ties!'

'Well, bring them with you! Put young Rodney on the pay-roll.'

'Well, he's got two GCEs!' I said.

'That don't matter. We'll think of something for him to do!'

My mind raced. I'd have to sort things out with my financial people. Lay off staff. Look out for a caretaker managing director for the Peckham office. Settle Rodney's newspaper bill. Say goodbye to Danny Driscoll . . .

'All right!' I said. 'Put it there, you old bastard. This is going to be a fast ride! Let's do it! Michael, champagne for me and my partner. See if you've got a bottle of Dillingers '75, Prince Charles' favourite.'

'No,' Jumbo said. 'That's Bollingers.'

'Rubbish,' I said. 'It's the best there is.'

When I outlined TITCO's new five-year business

plan to the board later that night, there was the odd voice of descent. But as soon as I showed Rodney a picture of the beach outside Jumbo's place in Sydney, he took about ten seconds to change his mind.

'Cor,' he said. 'Look at that bird!'

'Yeah, that would bruise your ribs, wouldn't it!' I said. 'That'll be us in a little while, Rodders. Blue skies, surfing, beach parties . . .'

Uncle Albert reckoned the only way to tell the difference between Aussie men and women was that the men spit further, but only just. As far as Rodney was concerned though, the camera never lied.

'It sounds great!' he said, his eyes still firmly fixed on the crumpet. 'And he wants us to help run his new car business?'

'Not *help* run it. I'm his partner, straight down the middle. He says he'll only take fifty-one per cent of the shares.'

'Well, how's that straight down the middle?'

I explained. 'I'll most probably have fifty-one per cent as well. Jumbo's going to stay behind the scenes and look after the money side of things, and I'm going to be sales director. My own executive office, with a swivel chair!'

'And what's my job?'

'You have got an absolutely vital role to play, Rodney, but I know you can handle it.'

'So what is it?' he asked, as if he wasn't totally convinced.

'When them Rollers and Mercedes come trundling off the boats, what is the one thing they're going to need?'

'Oh, got it! Import licences, customs clearance, all that.'

'It's much more important than that.'

He snapped his fingers. 'They need re-registering, new number plates and log books.'

I shook my head. 'There's something they need even more than that!'

He thought for a moment but simply lacked the vision.

'Cleaning!' I said.

'Cleaning? I'm going twenty thousand miles just to be a car cleaner?'

'No,' I said. 'Not just a car cleaner. You'll be a prestige car cleaner—and I've insisted you'll be in charge!'

'You mean I'll have staff working under me?'

'Eventually!' I said. 'This business is going to grow. A year from now and we won't be able to afford to have you downstairs with the mutton cloth and T Cut. You'll be needed in the boardroom. You'll have an in-car celluloid phone!'

'And a secretary?'

I could see that until I took that photo away from

him this conversation was destined to go round in circles. Sooner or later he was going to ask for a bedroom with a mirrored ceiling.

'It's a must,' I said.

Two weeks later I got the letter from Australia House telling me that there was always room for a top-of-the-range entrepruner in Godzown country, especially since my old mucker Blondie was about to be leaving a bit of a gap. I was well chuffed.

'You know, Del Boy,' Uncle Albert said that evening, 'I think this is the chance that's going to change your life!'

'I'm going to make it this time, Albert! You bloody see if I don't!'

Rodney shuffled in from the bedroom looking like he'd lost a shilling and found sixpence.

'What's the matter?' I said.

'Nothing. Nothing's the matter . . .'

'Oi, you're not getting homesick already?'

He handed me a piece of paper. 'Look, I got a letter this morning as well. They've refused me an immigration visa! They've turned me down! Sorry, Del . . .'

'But why, Rodney?' Uncle Albert said. 'You're young . . .'

'And you've got GCEs,' I added.

'I've also got a criminal record for an offence involving drugs!'

I was choked. 'Yeah, but . . . I mean . . . Bloody hell, that happened years ago! You had one bloody puff!'

'I'm sorry, Del, I'm really sorry. I've messed it all up for you, ain't I?'

I swallowed hard. 'No, you ain't, bruv. No, you ain't . . .'

'I have! I've blown your big chance.'

I could see it was time to remind him of what has become the byword of the Peckham Business School. I put my arm round his shoulder and said: 'There *is* a way round, Rodney! There's always a way round it!'

He brightened immediately. 'Really?'

'Yes,' I said. 'Don't worry, Rodney. I'll find another car cleaner!'

Somehow, this solution didn't appeal to him as much as you might think.

'You'll find *another* car cleaner? You mean you're still going? You're going without me?'

I suppose I shouldn't have been surprised that he went a bit lollopy.

'What can I do, Rodders? I've got a partnership over there!'

'But what about our partnership?'

'Our partnership?' For a moment there he lost me. 'Oh, *our* partnership! Well, of course, it means the whole world to me, Rodney, but I'm going to have to say *bonjour* to it!'

'Look boys,' Albert interrupted, 'I know it's none of my business . . .'

'Spot on, Albert!' Rodney said.

'I'll make the toast.'

When Albert had gone I made the sort of speech Blondie's going to have to make to his board of directors before he has it away on his toes back to Catford.

'This is a golden opportunity to fulfil my potential. And you expect me to give it up and stay here flogging this rubbish?' I waved at the current TITCO inventory. 'I've got twenty-four computers that don't work and a near-Persian rug that's got more food on it than a menu!'

Charity begins at home, but pretty soon it moves offshore.

'But last year when *I* had a golden opportunity you forced me to give it up, didn't you? All that cobblers about loyalty and family ties!'

'You wanted to become a window cleaner,' I said. 'I mean, it was hardly the end of the rainbow, was it?'

'At least I'd have had my own business.'

'But you've got your own business now!' I said. 'The moment I board the plane you will be the sole proprietor of Trotters Independent Trading Company!'

He didn't immediately see the potential. 'And what exactly am I supposed to trade with?'

'Well,' I said, 'to start with you've got these beautiful computers. A gorgeous deep-pile Persian rug—a quick sloosh with a J Cloth and it's a goer! And I'm leaving you my little black book, Rodders. It contains the names and addresses of all my birds!'

He took it without the ceremony I felt the occasion demanded.

'So this is my future. I've got two dozen computers that don't compute, the only rug in the world with a sell-by date and this.' He riffled the pages. 'The script for *A Hundred and One Dalmations*. Thanks a lot, Del.'

'Look, Rodney,' I said. 'Rodders . . . I could make a fortune over there! I've checked the exchange rates, everything. There are more dollars than pounds in Australia. I could be a millionaire this time in six months! I'll start sending you money any time after that!'

'You know, Del, I've got a feeling the real opportunity lies right here. What happens when a country's in a depression? Money gets tight, people can't afford inflated shop prices, so what do they do? They come to blokes like us. The more hard-up Britain gets, the richer we'd become!'

I was a bit gobsmacked. Rodney normally wanders around the corridors of the TITCO empire like a tit in hibernation, but this was pure Nigel Dawson. It must have tired him out, because he went to bed about five minutes later, leaving me to puff away on a Castella and think strategy.

After a couple of brandies and a spot of number-crunching I got on the dog to Jumbo in Sydney. He sounded a bit jet-logged. I looked at my watch. It was only half eight or so, but there you go. Some punters take to international travel like a pig to sugar; others just can't take the pace.

Rodney emerged a couple of hours later, looking a bit sheepish.

'All right?' he said.

'Yeah, brill!'

'I owe you an apology, Del. All them things I said earlier—I was right out of order. You've got to take that opportunity!'

I smiled at him. 'No, it's too late, bruv! I just phoned Jumbo and called the whole thing off.'

'You ain't! Oh, no! Was it anything I said?'

'Well, it was in a way, Rodney,' I said. 'You were going on about the real opportunity lying right here! The country's in a bad way, money's tight, people are looking for bargains—and who do they come to first?'

'Blokes like us!'

'Right!' I said. 'And I think you hit the nail bang on the head.' I gazed out the window for a moment, across the twinkling lights of Dockside Estate, past the

Herrington Road council bungalows, the cemetery and the welcoming neon of the Star of Bengal, to the horizon.

'Rodney, this wonderful land of ours is on the eve of a Golden Age of the black market! And me and you are there first. I'm glad I listened to you, Rodders. That chance of a lifetime could have ruined me!'

AFTERWARDS

....

As John and I put the finishing touches to *The Trotter Way to Millions*, a *bon motto* here, a *boeuf à la mode* there, he asked me if I have any regrets.

'None at all, my son,' I replied. 'None at all. Australia's twenty thousand miles away, and dialling from there don't half make your fingers ache. Rodders is well set up with that Cassandra, TITCO's on course for a few Stock Market flirtations and, well, here we are getting stuck into publishing. You know, this time next year we'll be millionaires!'